We Plough the Seas and Scatter

Further Adventures of a Priest in the Royal Navy

Michael Wishart

First published by Michael Wishart 2022
Copyright © Michael Wishart 2022
The moral right of the author has been asserted.
Some names have been changed.
Cover design Bogna Zwegrodzka
ISBN: 9798833313770
All rights reserved. Except in the case of brief quotations quoted in reviews or critical articles, no part of this book may be used or reproduced in any manner whatsoever without written permission from the author.

This book is dedicated to my wife, Laura, whose kindness is inexhaustible and whose advice I value so much but above all for putting up with me!

Also to the young men and women of the Royal Navy, the Royal Marines and the Royal Naval Reserve, whose lives I shared for a few years. I will always be grateful to them and proud of our service together.

Contents

Prologue …p1
Chapter 1: The Green Green Grass of Home …p3
Chapter 2: The Part-Time Navy …p5
Chapter 3: Echoes of a Distant War …p11
Chapter 4: Second Time Around? …p22
Chapter 5: Fair was the Wind to France …p25
Chapter 6: Pastures New …p35
Chapter 7: Pompey here we Come …p40
Chapter 8: While the Cat's Away …p42
Chapter 9: HMS Fife …p52
Chapter 10: O Islands in the Sun …p60
Chapter 11: If You Sail the Mediterranean You Must Call and See the Pope! …p74
Photographs …p83
Chapter 12: Istanbul and the Greek Islands …p97
Chapter 13: The Kingdom of Fife and the Pool of London …p101
Chapter 14: The Great Lakes and the Windy City …p104
Chapter 15: Fife's Farewell …p110
Chapter 16: 6th Frigate Squadron …p113
Chapter 17: A Caribbean Tragedy …p119
Chapter 18: HMS Nelson …p128
Chapter 19: HMS Collingwood …p140
Chapter 20: HMS Invincible …p149

Chapter 21: Orient Express '92 or
The Road to Hong Kong and Other Places ...p206
Chapter 22: HMS Excellent aka Whale Island ...p242
Chapter 23: HMS Osprey -- Portland
Naval Base ...p258
Epilogue: Not Quite the End ...p264
Acknowledgements ...p269

Foreword

This is a story of two lives, one is that of a parish priest, the other of a naval chaplain and we see Michael sometimes agonising over the choice between the two. There is a third dimension too, of course, and that is the responsibility of a family and the strain that seagoing and separation place on those bonds.

Michael's parish was in an idyllic rural setting but I suspect that, in the back of his mind, were his memories of his previous four years in the Royal Navy, perhaps made even more poignant by his continued links as a reservist and through his chaplaincy of a Naval Reserve establishment. The call back to the sea was always there in the background and eventually it won.

I was touched by his invitation for me to write a Foreword for this, his second book, as we served together three times, at sea and ashore, and I am very familiar with the other establishments he describes.

There are other links, too — Wales, the land of my birth, holidays on the Gower and a clear understanding of the contribution made by naval reservists through my father's 28 years of service. For those who have not served, here is a real insight into the life and times of a seagoing clergyman.

Uniquely among the British Armed Services, the naval chaplain holds no rank. While he or she is accommodated with the officers in the Wardroom, the chaplain's lack of rank allows access to all parts of the ship and its people at all levels. None of that access is a given, it must be won by patience, trust and discretion. To the ship's company, whether of a seagoing vessel or a shore establishment, he is their parish priest, with all that entails. Michael tells of many aspects of that role - baptisms, weddings, dealing with loss, separation and even suicide, as well as providing opportunities for worship but there is much more than that. Once that trust is won, the chaplain can also be an essential conduit into the mood and feelings of the ship's people and I always placed great store on his insight and advice, not least when dealing with the challenge of the introduction for the first time of women into sea going warships of the Royal Navy.

He describes with humour the many other, perhaps unexpected, elements of sea-going life – showing the flag, runs ashore, organising entertainment for the ship's company, fund-raising raffles and Royal visits, to name but a few.

After the variety and occasional glamour of a deployment in the flagship, Michael's next appointments ashore as he neared the end of his naval career presented different challenges but the pastoral care of his more disparate and less homogeneous flock was still his prime concern. Finally his time in the RN came to an end as he prepared to face other very different demands in his new parish back in Wales. His deep-rooted Christian faith is evident throughout this tale, wherever he served, together with his humour, determination, practicality and the thoughtful ways in which he introduced others to his beliefs. He offers a clear insight into what makes a good ship and asks himself whether he made a difference. There is absolutely no doubt in my mind that he did – in spades. Will there be a third volume to this story? I do hope so!

Rear Admiral John Tolhurst CB FRAeS

Prologue

Everyone in life experiences what's commonly called 'learning curves'. From the day we are born the learning curves are there – learning to walk, talk and all the other things that we take for granted but have to be learned. Learning curves are based upon the decisions we make and we make decisions every day in big and small ways.

Some are just everyday things, others have long-term implications which can protect and nurture the lives of children and act as a buttress to a failing relationship. As we get older those curves and decisions sometimes get steeper and then as we get older still the learning curves get less steep and tail away.

In my life I've had more than my fair share of learning curves, and not only as a child. Coming on the borderline of the 11-plus and going to a technical school, I faced the competitive nature of secondary education. I have to say I wasn't very bright and I didn't do terribly well. I left with no qualifications at all. So it was with good fortune that I managed to secure an apprenticeship with the Pressed Steel Company.

Going to work amongst men was a big curve that had to be learnt: when to speak and when not to speak, gauging people's moods and so on. For a boy of 16 it was not easy. Then at 18 perhaps the biggest learning curve was when, one Friday evening, God poked me in the ear and said, 'I have a job for you to do,' and the process of Ordination had begun.

It was not something that I aimed at or even considered but there it was. However, I still continued with my apprenticeship until I qualified as an electrician. I then had to work by day and study by night to get the O and A Levels I needed before I could be accepted at theological college. This for me was another major learning curve because it was a complete change of life including academic work. I was terrified at the prospect.

Then after ordination I secured an appointment as a curate on a council estate in Swansea. From there another learning curve was entering the Royal Navy, which I refer to in my previous book *Onward Christian Sailors*. That book ended with my leaving the Royal Navy and anticipating a return to parish life. Not on a council estate but instead to a very deeply rural part of Radnorshire. This too was a learning curve, I had absolutely no experience of living in the countryside or knowing the ways of its people but I was soon to find out.

Chapter One

The Green Green Grass of Home

The world is filled with exotic, glamorous places but I don't suppose that applies to Beguildy, a small hamlet in the county of Radnorshire.

To locate it, find Aberystwyth on the west coast of Wales and draw a line across, Beguildy will be just south of the line as you move across. It comprises a few houses, a Post Office cum shop, a pub, a school and a church that overlooks the hamlet from a ridge on the side of the hill. Its name means 'a shepherd's place' and there are a lot of sheep there.

It is a very beautiful spot in a very beautiful part of Wales, located right on the border with England, with Shropshire on one side of the river Teme and Wales and Radnorshire on the other. It was to this hamlet that we came to live. It formed the part of the Parish of Beguildy with Heyope and to that Parish I was Inducted on the 10 May 1980 having spent the previous 4 years in the Royal Navy. It was probably as far from the sea as you could get, but it was a lovely place to live, surrounded by beautiful countryside and with a magnificent Victorian vicarage to live in.

As for the parish, well, parishes are much the same

really, with the same underlying factors. I'm a great believer in visiting parishioners in their homes or sailors on their mess decks. It was drummed into me by my training incumbent, Haydn Moses. He used to demand 15 visits from me a week so it left me with a belief in visiting. There is a saying, 'a house-going parson makes for a churchgoing people' and I think there's an awful lot of truth in that.

Quite a number of people came to my Induction including my friend Ray Roberts who was now Chaplain of the Fleet, resplendent in his red cassock as an appointed Chaplain to the Queen. During the course of the 'bun fight' which followed the church service, Ray said to me, 'The Navy has not yet done with you, because I want you to take over at *HMS Cambria* as chaplain. The current chaplain has applied to join the Navy so I'd like you to take over from him. Make an appointment and call down to see them'. There it was again, the call of the sea but my immediate priority was my new parish and its people, and my family too of course!

Chapter Two

The Part-Time Navy

Though I could wax lyrical about the joys of country living, this narrative is not about rural parochial ministry. It's about my involvement with the Royal Navy. Because in the midst of parish and family life I had committed to becoming the chaplain of *HMS Cambria* in accordance with the request of the Chaplain of the Fleet. What it meant to me was that once a month I would drive to Cardiff to *HMS Cambria* which is the South Wales Division of the Royal Naval Reserve. At that time, it was based in the Custom House on the south dock in Cardiff.

My first visit to *Cambria* was a 'look see'. If it was not mutually acceptable then it would have gone no further. The outgoing chaplain was Godfrey Hilliard who had been a fellow student with me. He was now senior curate in the parish of Whitchurch in Cardiff and had been accepted into the Chaplain's Branch. Little did either of us know then but our paths were to cross on a number of occasions in the years that lay ahead.

Perhaps it might be helpful if I explain that *HMS Cambria* is, what's known in the Navy as, a 'stone frigate'. Like other establishments it has the prefix of *HMS* to show that it belongs to the Navy but it doesn't sail anywhere! However, at that time there was a ship attached to *Cambria* which did sail, *HMS St David*, a minesweeper which was moored not far away. Godfrey showed me over the ship and then introduced me to a lot of people who all made me feel very welcome. It was to be a very long association with *Cambria* which has only recently come to an end.

Although I knew a little bit about the workings of the Royal Navy I found myself on a fresh learning curve discovering the work of the Royal Naval Reserve. The entire Reserve was given over to the art of minesweeping which was, and remains, a hugely important task in the defence of shipping. Any maritime nation can have its entire trade threatened by mines which is a cheap and very effective way to bring about that threat. Mines are the deadliest form of hidden weapons and caused devastation during the world wars and other conflicts in between. Minesweeping remains a vital part of the naval life at sea and that the Naval Reserve had been given this task is a tribute to the dedication and skill of its people.

Cambria's sister establishment *HMS Flying Fox* in Bristol also had a minesweeper, *HMS Venturer* and they often worked in tandem. They were originally trawlers taken up from trade because they both had a large, steel A-frame on the stern which made them ideal vessels for what is known as 'deep arm sweep support', which means that they were able to reach to the very bottom and sweep any mine that was lying horizontally on the seabed.

HMS St David was to remain in Cardiff Docks but

Cardiff City Council wanted to redevelop the entire area so *Cambria* had to move. The only place that was on offer was a site at Sully Point some 8 miles to the west of Cardiff, which was leased by the Ministry of Defence for housing. Indeed, there were six officers' quarters built on the site and into these house we were to go. It was far from ideal but we had to make the best of it and we did. Eventually corridors linking some of the houses were constructed and the *Cambria* continued. Its location was the main problem as it was difficult to get to and as a result recruiting suffered. The Royal Marine Reserve decamped to Maindy Barracks in Cardiff which they shared with the Territorials, never an easy relationship! However, everything settled down and training continued over the years until *Cambria* had to move again, this time back to Cardiff because a brand new building was constructed, purpose built for the Reserve and recently commissioned as the 'new' *HMS Cambria*.

A few weeks after that first visit, having agreed to join the Reserve, I received a letter of appointment from the Chaplain of the Fleet, a letter of welcome from the Commanding Officer of *Cambria,* Captain John Price and a letter from the Bishop of Swansea and Brecon. Bishop Vaughn had given his permission. I then received a letter giving the location of the relocated *Cambria* and a map of how to get there but it was 'not easy'! It did become easier, I'm glad to say, as the years went by.

The weekly gatherings of the personnel were and still are known as Drill Nights. They took place on Monday and Wednesday evenings. I had to attend on a monthly basis so a routine quickly developed. I would leave the parish on a Wednesday afternoon, drive down through Breconshire and parts of Glamorgan to *Cambria* and then after the drill night had finished I would go on to Swansea to stay with my mother, travelling back to Beguildy the following day. I soon found out that there was a Naval Communications Training Centre in Swansea, based on the south dock. I was invited to visit them but they met on a Thursday evening so my monthly routine extended to include them and I returned home a day later.

Within the monthly visits there were the usual routines. On arriving at *Cambria* I would call on the Captain and then attend any meetings that were relevant to me and which would enable me to know what was going on within the establishment, what the future plans and programme were and how I fitted into them, if at all. After that, I would visit the different departments. Then 'Stand Easy' (a sort of tea break) would be piped, after which I would go around and talk to individuals, if they were able to spare the time from their normal duties and, of course, if they wanted to, because the chaplain is not always welcome!

When 'Secure' (the end of Drill Night) had been piped, there would be a drink or social time which could be in the wardroom or the senior ratings mess or on the drill deck where the junior ratings had their bar. It was always enjoyable, though at first it was somewhat fraught because I didn't know them and they didn't know me. I suppose one of the problems was the complete newness of it all, not only with different faces but with the newness of the surroundings which was affecting everyone. As the months went on things became easier as people got to know me and I them, so it became a meeting of friends rather than strangers.

There was inevitably an initial wariness because most of these young people had very little contact with the church and what they, more often than not, knew at all was either gleaned from newspapers or television or seeing a very strange person called 'a clergyman' in the street. I think it's fair to say the clergy have not always had a fair press either in the media or in the minds of the individual. Television programmes like *All Gas and Gaiters* which was popular at the time portrayed clergy as idiots, so barriers had to be overcome to enable me to present myself as a man doing a job of work for God. Now, if they didn't believe in God then that was OK, I would talk to them anyway but if they did believe in God then it made life a lot easier. It was exactly the same on board a ship visiting mess decks.

The 'new' relocated *Cambria* began to grow on us. The minesweeper remained in Cardiff Docks and training went on board there too. The aim was always to get as many people to sea as often as possible because the art of minesweeping had to be practiced and the only way to do that was weekend training. This meant that the ship was at sea every weekend. From Friday evening to Sunday evening the people were sailors learning how to carry out a dangerous job under difficult conditions. They would then return to harbour on Sunday evening in time to return to their normal civilian work.

It was the Navy in microcosm because every branch of the Royal Navy was represented within *HMS Cambria*. Year on year people got promoted, went on courses, left and joined. That's the sort of general outline of the routines that I and others followed but in addition, in order to qualify for the 'Bounty' (the pay that we received for being in the Naval reserve) not only did I have to attend Drill Nights each month but spend two weeks each year training. A requirement which applied to all. In my case, since I had spent the last 4 years in the RN there was a willingness to let me do things on my own. Normally what would happen is that an RNR chaplain would report to one of the base port areas and be under the direction of the chaplain RN there but because I had previous experience, the Chaplain of the Fleet was happy to let me run establishments unsupervised, which enabled the resident chaplain to go on leave. However, two major events took place and the call of the sea started to grow again.

Chapter Three

Echoes of a Distant War

The first of these came in April 1982 when the Argentinians invaded the Falkland Islands and what's become known as the Falklands War commenced. At the time I recalled a comment made to me by the RSM of 40 Commando, Bill Flatt. We were in the middle of Salisbury Plain and his words were, 'What we need is a small war just to focus the minds of the military and the public'. He got his wish. I also reflected that if the disastrous Defence cuts proposed by the then Secretary of State, John Nott, had gone ahead we would not have been able to muster a couple of rowing boats let alone the Task Group that the Navy quickly organised.

The ships sailed with some 'jingoism' and a lot of apprehension mingled with the hope that the Argentinians would go home and there would be no hostilities. In the meantime, I wrote to the Chaplain of the Fleet, Raymond Roberts, and asked to be recalled but there was no mechanism to call up the Reserve unless it was for a national emergency, which this was not. That mechanism exists now but not then, so my frustration grew. However, in preparation for casualties a reporting system was set up whereby families could be informed as quickly as possible. They were called Casualty Action Cells. Manned by Naval personnel, including chaplains, they were located at the main base port areas of Portsmouth, Plymouth, Chatham and Rosyth. I would assume that the other services had similar organizations. These were created so that in the event of casualties in the South Atlantic, reports would be sent to the action cells and information passed on to the families concerned.

I received a phone call from the Casualty Action Cell in Plymouth to ask that if the need arose would I be prepared to visit families in my area and inform them of injuries or death to their loved ones serving in the Royal Navy in the South Atlantic? I said if they knew of any sheep in the Falklands who had relatives in my parish I would gladly go and tell them. My sense of humour fell flat with the Wren officer to whom I was speaking. However recovering the situation, I said of course I would willingly go and visit families but bearing in mind my location I thought it unlikely. How wrong I was.

On 4 May 1982 HMS Sheffield, a Type 42 destroyer, was on radar picket duty when she was attacked by aircraft of the Argentinian Navy and struck by an Exocet missile. The ship was badly damaged and eventually abandoned only to drift for six days. Several attempts were made to see if she could be salvaged but on 10 May she rolled over and sank, taking with her the bodies of the 26 sailors who had died in the attack. One of whom was from south Wales.

As I said earlier, Drill Nights were on Monday and Wednesday each week and it just so happened that that particular week I could not attend drill on the Wednesday so, instead, went to *Cambria* on Monday 10 May. This was somewhat fortuitous.

A 200-mile exclusion zone had been declared around the Falklands and any Argentine shipping within the zone would be liable to be attacked. On Saturday the Argentinian cruiser, *Belgrano* had entered the exclusion zone and had been sunk by torpedoes launched by the submarine HMS Conqueror with great loss of life.

The shooting war had begun.

The Task Group had by now entered the area around the Falkland Islands and in retaliation Argentina hit the *Sheffield* and she went down on 10 May.

That evening after the Drill Night was over I was in a very crowded wardroom when I was called to the porter's lodge to take a phone call from the Casualty Action Cell in Plymouth asking me to go at once and visit a family at Aberavon, Port Talbot. The family home of one of the sailors killed in the attack. His name was Kevin Williams and he was just 20 years of age. Their home was on the Sandfields Estate in the town which covered a huge area. I readily agreed to go and left *Cambria* immediately.

My knowledge of Aberavon was sketchy to say the least and I had no map. It was, by now, dark and I arrived an hour later but where was the street? I followed the signs for the police station but when I got there it was closed. So I drove around hoping to see a street sign, I was sending up 'arrow prayers' asking for God's guidance, which worked. I pulled over to the kerb, got out and went up a garden path, knocked on the door. Eventually, through the glass in the door, a frail figure came shambling down the hall and an elderly lady came to the door but didn't open it. She said, 'I'm not going to open the door, who is it and what do you want?' I said, 'That's fine, I'm a clergyman and I'm looking for family in a particular street', which I named. She told me that it was second along on the right. My prayers had been answered, I had the help I asked for!

Having found the street, I located the house and went up the garden path. I was trying to get my thoughts into some sort of order. The first thing was to make sure that I had the right person, after all, Williams is not an uncommon name in Wales.

There is a set procedure regarding breaking the news of death in the Service and it usually involves a senior officer, who actually breaks the news, and then the Naval social worker and chaplain move in to help, and the officer withdraws. But here I was on my own with little authority. True, I had my ID Card and the telephone number of the Cell and that would have to suffice. So, with great apprehension I knocked on the door. It was eventually opened by a young man who asked me who I was and what I wanted. I said, 'Is this the home of Mrs Williams, if so I would like to speak with her'. He went into the house and Mrs Williams came to the door and asked what I wanted. I said, 'May I come in please, as what I have to say is very sensitive and I'm sure you would not want to discuss it in earshot of your neighbours'. Reluctantly she let me in and we went into the living room where *Pot Black* was on the television. I asked the young man to turn it off. I said, 'My name is Wishart and I am the chaplain to *HMS Cambria* and I have been instructed to visit you'. 'Are you Mrs Williams, the mother of Kevin Williams currently serving in *HMS Sheffield*?' 'Yes.' 'Then I am so very sorry to have to inform you that your son is missing, believed killed in action. Please accept my deepest sympathy'.

It took a moment before she began to break down in tears. The young man disappeared and some minutes later Mr Williams came in declaring that his son couldn't be dead as he could swim. I did not have the heart to tell him how Kevin had died. All I said was, 'The Casualty Action Cell will be in contact with further details in due course and if there's anything that we in *HMS Cambria* can do, then please let us know,' and I gave them my calling card.

As the family gathered and I began to take my leave, Mrs Williams said to me that she was worried about her father who was very close to Kevin; his name was Mr. Smith. I asked for his address and said that I would go and see him in the morning as it was far too late tonight.

The following morning I knocked on Mr Smith's door. When it opened I was faced by an elderly gentleman whose eyes were filled with tears.

'Come in,' he said. 'I understand that you were in the

Navy. It's good of you to call and see me'. He then broke down and I comforted him as best I could until he had recovered. I gazed around at an immaculate house, very well kept and looked after. Mr. Smith had been a 'matelot' and it showed. It was his influence that encouraged his grandson to join the Navy and he was so proud of him.

It seems that *HMS Sheffield* had been on patrol in the Persian Gulf and was returning home. On reaching Gibraltar Kevin sent a postcard to his grandfather saying he would soon be home but after posting the card, the ship up was ordered to join the Task Group and sailed south. Kevin, of course, never returned home.

I remained with Mr Smith for the bulk of the morning while he talked about his time in the Navy. Now his future was bleak. I said a prayer with him before I left. It was a heartbreaking situation and a very sad duty done. I returned home later that day in a very sombre mood.

Just four weeks later, on Saturday 12 June 1982 *HMS Glamorgan* was supporting 42 commando in the assault on the Two Sisters Hills overlooking Port Stanley when she was struck by a land-based Exocet missile, causing serious damage and casualties. Being so close to the end of the conflict it was such a shame that these men were hurt or killed. On the evening of Sunday, 13 June I received a phone call at the Vicarage asking me to go to Cardiff to visit a family whose son had been killed in that action. I refused on the principle that it was so late in the evening and it would take me several hours to get there.

As the crow flies it's only about 75 miles but going

round hills on country roads would take me quite a lot longer than a crow and this was going to be the last night's sleep that family would have in a while. So I suggested that I go down first thing the following morning. The Wren officer was quite adamant that I had to go that night, as there were worries that the newspapers would publish details before the families were informed. I pointed out that the newspapers by this time had already 'gone to bed' and nothing would be published before noon the following day but she was adamant that it had to be that night. I asked her to leave it with me and I would get my commanding officer to inform them. I telephoned my commanding officer who was in the middle of a dinner party and, after I explained the reason for the call, he said that he would go immediately which he did, after he donned his uniform. Early next morning around about 0600 the phone rang in the vicarage, it was the Casualty Action Cell wanting to know what was going on. When I asked why they said, 'We've just had the family on the phone asking for news of their son'. I said, 'I know exactly what's happened, leave it with me and I will be down there as soon as I possibly can'. So I shaved, showered and dressed, grabbed some breakfast, jumped in the car on my way to Cardiff. It was 0645. I had the family's address and I had a map but since time was of the essence, I went to the local police station and asked for guidance. They were very kind and placed at my disposal a police car which guided me to the family's home without sirens or lights.

I knocked on the door and a lady answered who, it transpired, was the deceased's sister. I asked if this was the home of Mr and Mrs Perkins and she said that it was. She asked me in and as I went into the hall an elderly gentleman was coming down the stairs. He smiled at me and asked, 'Are you from the Navy?' and I said that I was. He said, 'I knew there would be news soon, please come in'. I can see the scene in my mind still, he and Mrs Perkins sat on the sofa and the daughter stood behind, tense, as if she knew what was coming. I was indeed about to destroy their lives. I said, 'There are a couple of formalities', so I introduced myself and I asked them if they could confirm that they were the parents of Terence Perkins currently serving on board *HMS Glamorgan* in the South Atlantic and they said they were. Then came the bombshell, 'I'm very sorry to have to tell you that your son has been killed in action. Please accept our deepest sympathies'.

At first they looked puzzled, they said 'But that very nice man, the Captain, came from *HMS Cambria* last night and told us that there might be some good news'. I replied, 'I'm very sorry but during the night the news that came was not good, so I regret that your son has been confirmed killed in action'.

They collapsed, utterly distraught. Their daughter quietly said to me, 'I wondered last night whether in fact this was the case'. I replied, 'Well, messages can get confused when more people get involved in them, so sadly it's been a very sad duty for me'.

I stayed with them for the bulk of the day, giving them what comfort I could and to other members of the family as they arrived. I discovered that they were a church family, so I went to see the local vicar and explained the circumstances to him and he quickly informed the churchwardens and other members of the church, who could also give them support.

Late in the afternoon it being a Monday, it was a Drill Night in *Cambria,* so I went straight there. I went to the Captain's office and his secretary said, 'He won't be able to see you'. 'Would you care to bet on that?' I replied and knocked on the door and entered. I said, 'Sir, what happened?' and he looked suitably abashed and said, 'I couldn't do it, I had to give them some hope'.

I understood his dilemma, especially if breaking the news of death is a new experience but I said, 'Sadly, the truth is, if there is no hope, give no hope because all it does is lengthen the hurt and the sense of loss'. We all learned lessons from that incident. Yet again, I went home in a sombre mood.

Curiously, in 1992, Channel 4 produced a programme *The Falklands 10 Years On*, and the Perkins family were featured. They mentioned 'that nice Captain who came to see us' but I received not a word, not that I wanted any, I was just doing a part of my job. We may not shoot messengers but we can wipe them from our memories.

After these incidents parish life was very welcome. It contained the usual things of visiting, services, sermon preparation and the like and yes, the occasional funeral too. But the Navy was never very far away and a few weeks later I travelled to Plymouth to carry out my 2 weeks reserve training at *HMS Thunderer,* located in the north of the city at the Royal Naval Engineering College, Manadon. Once again I was allowed to carry out my two weeks training unsupervised, which enabled the chaplain to have a very well-deserved break. Like a number of establishments there was a f4-term year with leave taken at the usual times but when there was an active church congregation within the establishment it meant the chaplain had difficulty taking leave at the usual times.

My time in Manadon quickly passed and I returned to my parish but Naval occasions were_coming thick and fast because the next thing to come along was a wedding. It was the venue_for this wedding that was quite important. The groom had applied to be married in the crypt of St. Paul's Cathedral in London! Some weeks before, I received a phone call from the Dean of St. Paul's asking if I knew of an Anthony Syrett who had applied for a wedding there. Tony's father was a member of Order of the British Empire and members have the right for their sons to be married in the crypt of St. Paul's. I had served with Tony on board *HMS Berwick.*

Those of you who have read my previous book may find that interesting because Tony, having been married before, met up with a former friend from his days in university, an American lady called Annie Yancey and had begun a new relationship. She was, I believe, working in the American Embassy in London and when we went to Houston in Texas, she flew out and became an invaluable guide for tours around the city. Before I left the ship at Houston they kindly asked if I would conduct their wedding whenever it would be arranged and I readily agreed. Little did I know that it was going to happen in the crypt at St. Paul's. So when the Dean phone me up I thought he was going to offer me a job but that was not to be! However, I was able to assure him that Tony and Annie were honourable people.

It seemed that the cathedral was being used for the wrong reasons with many people's sole reason for applying for marriage there was so that they could have their wedding photographs taken on the steps of St. Paul's. When I assured him that Tony and Annie were having a small wedding and to them it was the ceremony not the photographs that mattered, he agreed. The wedding took place on the 28 August and it was a splendid occasion.

Chapter Four

Second Time Around?

Parish life continued, as did my visits to *Cambria*. It was at a planning meeting there that the second big reason to re-join the Navy came about.

There was to be a New Entry Cruise. This is when those who had recently joined would be given the opportunity to spend time at sea and experience, for the first time, life on board a ship. The minesweeper *HMS St. David* would be used to teach sailors things like watch keeping, basic firefighting and so on. Though this was not to be a minesweeping exercise, this too would be explored outside the classroom. It was suggested that it might perhaps be a good idea for me to be part of the new entry cruise given my background, which was great for me, as it was an opportunity to get to know the sailors who had recently joined over a consistent period of time. I had never sailed in a minesweeper, they were much smaller ships than the ones I'd been used to, so it was going to be a new experience for me too.

Over the next few weeks the plans for this cruise were becoming finalized. There would be four officers on board. The Captain was to be Lieutenant Commander Tony Mason, a delightful man and a very experienced follow my heart. In the years that lay ahead I would be incumbent of two parishes; help build a new church and community hall in one and raise thousands of pounds to preserve medieval churches in another but now God was leading me back to the sea. At least, that's what I hoped and prayed was the case.

Chapter Seven

Pompey here we Come

The city of Portsmouth is the most populous part of the United Kingdom. Built on an isthmus, it has been a centre of maritime activity for many centuries. It was on Portsdown Hill overlooking Portsmouth that Henry VIII witnessed the capsizing of the Mary Rose which stalled the beginnings of a standing Navy.

Portsmouth has a long and illustrious connection with the sea and it is no surprise that a royal dockyard was created and expanded as the Navy expanded. The Dockyard is still huge, with many historic buildings, the oldest being the Ropewalk, built in 1774. It was here that the ropes were made and pulled out at one end by horses to service the ships needs for rigging.

Next door to the Ropewalk is the church of St. Ann's. Built in 1776, it has served the spiritual need of sailors and dockyard workers down the centuries and still continues to do so. During the Second World War the church, like the rest of the dockyard, was bomb damaged, with the North Wall of the church almost entirely destroyed, but when the war was over the decision was made rebuild and renovate. The North window has a very modern Christ-like figure standing over the dockyard, I always thought it looked like Sting from the pop group 'The Police' but it is a beautiful building, with a balcony and a very impressive interior. Around its walls are plaques and memorials highlighting the history of the Royal Navy and its involvement in the city of Portsmouth.

People have very mixed attitudes to Portsmouth. For example, my friend Ray Roberts likened Portsmouth to the 'East Berlin of the south coast', but I loved the city and we were to live there for eleven years.

I returned to the Navy on 12 February 1985 and my appointment was to St Ann's as Assistant Chaplain. My boss was Michael Henley who had been staff Chaplain during my first 4 years. He was a delightful, affable man whom I liked greatly. The chaplaincy was contained within the church complex because an extension had been built which contained a choir robing room, a verger's office and the chaplain's office with a smaller office for the assistant. My friend, Godfrey Hilliard, was the assistant but he was due to take up his appointment as chaplain to *HMS Intrepid*. We would work together for the next few weeks, though, so that I would be familiar with the specifics of the role. This would be no easy task as Godfrey was good at his job.

As a family we moved to a married quarter in Pembroke Park, Southsea and received a very warm welcome. The small but loyal congregation in St Ann's comprised mainly retired Naval personnel and their wives or widows. The numbers were always increased when we had an Association Sunday, that's when ship's associations had their reunions in Portsmouth and came to church on a Sunday morning. On those occasions the congregation could swell to a couple of hundred. St Ann's Church was in effect a Naval parish church and we had all the usual services that went with it.

The working day began with Morning Prayer followed by Holy Communion and ended with Evensong, depending on where we were during the course of the afternoon. The church was locked in the evening and opened up in the mornings including Saturdays. Weddings, of which there were more than a few, were conducted by Special Licence only. They were confined to serving Naval personnel or their daughters. I have no idea why it was daughters only but that's the way it was and Special Licenses had to be applied for to the Archbishop of Canterbury.

More often than not there was a reluctance to issue the licence because a lot of people whose fathers have been in the Navy were living miles and miles away and living in somebody else's parish, so we had to have letters from the parish priest saying that he'd seen the people involved and approved the wedding. It was a very complex administrative process and there were a lot of them.

We had funerals too. Sometimes conducted from the church but mainly the Committal of Cremated Remains of former sailors or marines to the deep. There is an organization set up within the Navy to assist families who request to have their loved one's ashes committed in this way. I personally conducted 120 Committals of Ashes in a year!

The newly appointed Bishop of Portsmouth, Timothy Bavin had no real jurisdiction over us but it was courteous to call upon him and introduce ourselves. He was to become a friend to the Naval chaplains in the Dockyard and I liked him very much. He conducted the Confirmation service in St. Ann's at which my children were confirmed.

I've always believed that visiting is one of the essences of the parish life when we can get to know people more fully and encourage them in the Christian Faith. Working in St Ann's was no different. We visited various parts of the dockyard quite regularly. It was always a joy to go to the coppersmith shop for example and have a cup of tea and talk to people, many of whom had worked in the Dockyard for years. It was fascinating to hear their stories. We also visited ships that were alongside who did not have a chaplain, or ships that were in refit. There was also a visiting of sailor's homes.

We had a large number of enquiries regarding baptisms and I would always arrange to visit their homes and not just take details in the office. From such visits we had quite a few Confirmation candidates. We saw the congregation begin to grow, so that instead of 20 or 30 people on a Sunday we might have 60. When the associations joined us the church was packed.

Of the ships in the dockyard, one which never went

to sea was *HMS Victory*. This magnificent ship where Nelson died was the flagship of the fleet that was victorious at the Battle of Trafalgar and remains the flagship of Commander-in-Chief Fleet. Though not seaworthy, *Victory* was actually a working warship. At that time, she had a ship's company of sailors and marines who were either injured and were awaiting rehabilitation or they were waiting for a 'draft' to a new ship or they were going outside. But it was a full working ship's company and they conducted the tours of the ship as well as their other duties.

Chaplains conducted prayers at divisions on a regular basis as well as other services like baptisms and the Christmas Carol Service which was hugely popular and very well attended, with the choir of St Ann's leading the singing. Being on the second gun deck with lanterns lit and with the smell of tar and cordage it all went to make the carol service very emotive.

I also conducted a number of baptisms on board *Victory* because those serving in a ship have the right to have their babies baptised in the ship's bell and the names engraved on the rim of the bell. For historic reasons this could not be done with *Victory*'s bell. Instead, a brass plaque recording the baptism was placed on the deck head beams. There are a number of those brass plaques which bear my name and I'm very proud to have served the sailors and their families in that capacity.

St Ann's had a very good organist and choir with a full range of male and female voices and a number of younger voices too. Three new members joined in the form of my children, who were made very welcome. They enjoyed this new experience and their musical knowledge was expanded greatly.

So life was quite full and busy for us all and it was a happy time. Each summer, to coincide with the August Bank holiday weekend, 'Navy Days' took place when the dockyard was open to the public so that they could explore the yard and the ships. It was hugely popular and thousands of visitors came from far and near. St. Ann's was very much a part of 'Navy Days', the church was open to visitors, we had special services and we also set up cake stalls and tea tents, with members of the congregation baking cakes and making sandwiches. Many coach drivers directed their passengers to come to St. Ann's for their refreshments and all the monies raised went to charity. This lasted a number of years until the traders in other parts of the dockyard complained that we were taking their trade away, which we really didn't want to do but it was inevitable, and so we had to scale back.

Eventually Navy Days shrank and disappeared but they were great days when the congregation worked closely together and it had a knock on effect on our Sunday attendance and worship.

The chaplaincy had the use of a garden which had never been looked after and was a complete and utter mess. Having taken over the 'new' premises in the autumn of 1985 during that winter I organized a working party on a Saturday morning to clear out the rubbish to try to make it useable. I had arranged a skip which was delivered on the Friday afternoon but overnight it snowed! It rarely snows in Portsmouth but it did on that night. About half a dozen men turned up including Admiral Barker and a leading Seaman, whose baby was to be baptised and who became regular members of St Ann's. Between us we pulled down the old chicken sheds and cleared the site. We worked from 0900 until midday despite the snow. It was very cold but we got the job done so I reckoned that it deserved a good tot of rum. We adjourned to the Pembroke Arms in Old Portsmouth and had a number of double rums to restore circulation. It was fascinating watching an admiral and a leading seaman socialising. St Ann's was certainly breaking down barriers!

Over the next few months, the garden was laid and a barbecue constructed and the chaplaincy and its garden became well used.

Chapter Eight

While the Cat's Away...

The other major event in our time at St. Ann's was the bi- centenary celebrations. Having been built in in 1776, the building was to be 200 years old. Michael had gone on leave to Scotland. He said, 'Try and see what we can do by way of preparation'.

The first thing I did was to speak to the manager of the Naval Museum shop. I explained what we wanted and he said that there was quite a range of merchandise that could be attractive memorabilia but it takes time for orders to come through. Using my initiative, I ordered a number of tasteful items including a pen and ink drawing of the church. One of the other things I did was to contact the Post Office with a view to having every letter that left Portsmouth franked with a silhouette of St. Ann's church and the dates either side. This brought an enormous response from people all over the world. We had letters from people who served in the dockyard doing the war for whom it brought back so many memories.

We also held a celebratory cocktail party which came about in this way. Michael was still on leave and yet again it snowed in Portsmouth. I received a phone call in the morning from the Admiral's secretary asking me if I would go for lunch. Because of the snow, lots of people had cried off and she wanted substitutes. The Admiral was Sir Peter Stanford who had been in charge of the 3rd Flotilla when I served in the 7th Frigate Squadron. It was he who had ordered a friend and I out of the Officers Club in Gibraltar in disgrace. He and Lady Stanford were regular Communicants at St Ann's. I duly presented myself for lunch. There was a roaring fire in the grate and the only others present were the Admiral's secretary and a Lieutenant Commander who was a little bit on the nervous side.

We sat down to dine and Lady Stanford asked me how the preparations were going for the celebrations. Sir Peter had a big gruff voice and mutton chop whiskers and his voice was very much like that of the Admiral from the radio programme 'The Navy Lark'. He said, 'What can I do to help?' and I said, 'Would it be possible for the church to have an event on board *HMS Victory*?' 'What did you have in mind?' 'A cocktail party which would be a gesture of thanks to all those people who have supported us during the bi-centenary celebrations, an opportunity to say, 'Come and have a drink with us'. It would be the penultimate event as we have the Service of celebration the following day.' 'Good idea,' he said, 'make it so'.

He looked at Lady Stanford who nodded in agreement and then he said, 'Who's going to pay for it?' and I said after some hesitation, 'Well, you are Sir, it was your suggestion after all.' I thought, 'He's kicked me out before so I suppose he could do it again,' but he said, 'Damned chaplains, they catch you every way', and his wife, at the other end of the table, smiled and said, 'Well, darling, you did offer,' and he said, 'Yes, I did didn't I. OK make that so too!'

When Michael came back from leave he said, 'What on earth have you been doing? I've just had the Admiral's secretary on the phone asking about potential numbers for a cocktail party?'

On 14 July our Amport Conference was held and I was told that I was to leave St Ann's and go back to sea as chaplain to *HMS Fife*. This filled me with some apprehension as I had never before served in a single ship, but I looked forward to it for I believe that the Naval chaplain is more effective at sea.

That Amport was also memorable because I met a fellow Welshman named Mark Jackson who had recently joined the Branch. He came down the pub with us one evening and we stayed too long. On our return to the house we found the doors locked but a window in the chapel had been left open. Had we rung the doorbell we could have incurred the Chaplain of the Fleet's wrath, so casting our eyes around they fell on young Mark who was the youngest and slimmer than the rest of us. A unanimous decision was taken and Mark was chosen to rescue us. He was hoisted up through the window and, losing his hand hold, crashed to the floor. He could have been badly hurt if he had collided with a church chair, for they were sturdily made, but he didn't. I suppose he could have left us standing there but being the generous soul that he was, he let us in. He still bleats about being 'dragooned' into committing a 'break in'. He went on to great things and is still a dear friend.

The time rolled by and the week of celebration arrived, all the arrangements worked splendidly. All letters from Portsmouth were duly franked, the merchandise arrived intact and went on sale. The cocktail party was a roaring success. It's the only time I've ever seen my mother really 'squiffy'. She had been drinking 'Horse's Necks' and the stewards, who were my very best friends, had plied her with drinks because she was my mum.

Next day, the Sunday, was my last official day in St Ann's. It was also the culmination of the celebration with a special service and the church was packed. The Bishop of Portsmouth preached and celebrated Holy Communion and people who had served in the dockyard and St Ann's came back to be part of it. On completion, a celebratory lunch was held on the lawn at Admiralty House. There was even a celebratory cake baked by the chefs in *Nelson*. Which everyone enjoyed on that glorious July day. It was a most fitting celebration for a church that had served the Navy for so long.

It was said that Michael and I had been too successful in St Ann's. So much had taken place in such a short time, just 18 months, but perhaps the best thing was seeing the Sunday congregation grow to a regular 60 - 70 souls, excluding the Sunday School. It wasn't difficult, just visiting and being open to the opportunities as they arose. Either way, Michael was appointed to St Margaret's, the base church at *HMS Cochran* or HM Naval Base, Rosyth and I was appointed chaplain to *HMS Fife*. Back to sea for me, I would miss St Ann's but my family would continue to worship there and no doubt I would pop in from time to time.

Chapter Nine

HMS Fife

HMS *Fife* was a guided missile Destroyer launched in 1964 and commissioned in 1966. She had a busy life including sailing on a round-the-world deployment in 1970, in company with other ships. It was said that Lord Louis Mountbatten had a hand in her design and that she was originally classed as a Cruiser. However, the Ministry of Defence no longer built cruisers, so 20 feet was chopped off the bows and she was called a Destroyer, which is why the front end of the ship had a very 'stubby' look.

Her main armament was a Sea Slug missile system. It appeared that the ship had been built around the entire missile system, its magazines and launchers. In 1985 she began a major refit when the missile systems and magazines were dismantled and removed, creating extra space with compartments below decks, which were converted into classrooms and accommodation for the Officer Cadets and Apprentices who would be joining the ship. A navigational training classroom was constructed aft of the ship on the site of the Sea Slug missile launchers and the helicopter was changed from a 'Wessex 3' to the more versatile 'Lynx'. The navigation training classroom became known as 'the hut' because that's what it looked like, a metal box stuck on the back of the ship but it was very effective. *Fife* became the Dartmouth Training Ship and that's when I joined her, just after she had come out of refit.

My appointment was from 26 August but a few days before, I moved some kit on board mainly to see what accommodation I had been allocated. I have to say I wasn't greeted with any great enthusiasm, which set the tone for my relationship with the command and the executive. I don't think any thought had been given to a chaplain at all. I assumed that they had not been told that I was arriving. Anyway, I was eventually given a cabin on the wardroom flat. A flat in a warship is an area outside offices or compartments. This particular flat had a screen door opening out onto the main deck on one side and a ladder on the other side descending onto the main companionway, which ran the length of the ship and was known as 'The Great Glen'. Opposite my door was the front door of the wardroom. Also opening out onto the flat was the Commander's cabin and the Chief Steward's office. It was a very busy place but the advantage was that anyone could call to see me without having to travel through 'officer country'. Mine was a double cabin and I suspect it had been allocated to me as an afterthought but the location was excellent.

Unfortunately, the cabin was a tip, it had been used as a storage/dumping ground during the refit and nobody had seen fit to clean it out. I went to the chief steward and said, 'Would it be possible for my cabin to be sorted out please before I move on board?' The Petty Officer Steward seemed reluctant to do anything because I found out that he had been using the cabin as his own private space, so I had to be a bit emphatic, stating that I wanted it done by the weekend because I was bringing my kit on board. With great reluctance it was done. Joining routines are pretty standard and I did the usual things like getting a laundry number and a mess number, calling on the Captain and wandering about the ship. Nobody showed me around but I knew the back end from the front.

Being on board *Fife* was, for me, a strange experience because she was a very big ship compared to a frigate, with many more people on board, so much so, that Fife was the last ship to sling hammocks. About a dozen officer cadets had to sleep in hammocks as there was a paucity of accommodation. It didn't seem to bother them and it made 'Navy News', which pleased the Captain.

The wardroom was enormous in terms of numbers, not only ship's officers but training staff from Dartmouth and *HMS Sultan,* the mechanical engineering school. I began in the usual way by visiting the Master-at-Arms office (the police station) and obtaining a list of the presidents and 'killicks' of the messes (a killick is a Leading Hand which is the Navy's version of corporal in charge) and I began to visit them in their places of work to say hello and to find out whether I could visit their messes at their convenience.

I had a wonderful reception, far better from the Senior

and Junior ratings than I did from the Wardroom, so that lifted my spirits. It is perhaps worth mentioning at this point that unlike a priest in a normal parish who receives support from a church council or regular members of a congregation, the chaplain is not guaranteed any support. The chaplain is at the cutting edge of evangelism and you have to be prepared to 'fight your corner' constantly. The ship's company were young, boisterous and pretty agnostic, which made mess deck visiting a really enjoyable challenge.

We sailed for Portland to be tested. *Fife* had just come out of refit and therefore had a 'new' ship's company who had to be put through their paces. Portland was the home of Flag Officer Sea Training (FOST) and his staff, it was their job to initiate all sorts of emergencies on board the ship to test the capability of the ship's company and how it responded to those tests. For example, how to deal with a fire or man overboard or accidents or emergencies or damage control. All of these and more are used to test the ship, including something called 'Exercise Awkward' where the ship would come under attack from both land and sea. Operational Sea Training was vitally important to the good order, fighting efficiency and well-being of the ship and its people but it was faced with a little bit of dread because you didn't know what was coming or when it would come but everybody worked hard to ensure that we got at least a satisfactory pass. We would be in Portland for at least two weeks at sea and alongside. I'd not been through basic sea training before and I didn't have a clue as to what to expect but I managed.

The first Sunday on board I had a 1000 service, a hymn, prayer sandwich sort of thing, followed by shortened Holy Communion. It was pretty poorly-attended and I later discovered that it was declared to be a working day. Nobody had told me. As the Commander would not be flexible in timings, church services had to be fitted in with the rest of the daily routine. This meant that everyone was working and unable to get to church even if they wanted to, thus defeating the object of me being there. That's what I was going to face more than once during my time in the ship. Nobody said it would be easy and I had to work with whatever I'd been given. The band we had on board was a volunteer band under the baton of a Band Sergeant Royal Marines who was absolutely superb and they were a great support.

During the following week we were put through our paces including 'Exercise Awkward'. I attached myself to the sick bay on these occasions and assisted the upper deck casualty team who went out and brought in 'casualties' who were very well made up to look as though they had real wounds and injuries, with lots of blood and bits hanging off. The FOST team also included medics who knew their stuff so the makeup was most effective. If Action Stations were for real, as I didn't have a specific place, my role was a roving one, which enabled me to go from place to place and give encouragement to the troops. But on exercise, my presence in the casualty team was very well received.

The following Sunday we were alongside in Portland and I, like the rest of the ship's company, had to get off because there was going to be a major fire exercise to test the fire brigade's response to a fire. A ship is one of the most difficult places to fight a fire and it made sense if the people were not there. Only the duty watch remained.

The following day we sailed for the Portsmouth where we would be alongside for at least the next two weeks prior to sailing for the Caribbean deployment.

We sailed for the Caribbean on 29 September at 0900. The ship was pretty full with the normal ship's company plus the officers under training and the apprentices, many of whom were going to sea for the first time, and a goodly number still had exams to take. Members of the ship's company required 'O' and 'A' Levels for advancement, so I once again found myself in the role of teaching English and History but also marking journals.

The office cadets had to keep a journal, a sort of diary in which they wrote essays on topics given by their divisional officer, usually about what they have been doing on board ship or where they had been or what they intended to do. I and other Heads of Departments were tasked with marking these journals and interviewing the young gentlemen as to their comments. It made for very interesting reading and I got to know them fairly quickly.

The day after we sailed, when we were off Portland, there was a gun exercise because *Fife* still had a turret with twin 4.5 inch guns and space for Exocet missile pods. Although I don't think we had any missiles on board we did have ammunition for the guns, so the guns were fired before we made a slow passage to Mounts Bay, in Cornwall, for an exercise in landing Sea King helicopters on our deck.

Two days out and I was sent for by the Commander and asked to take on the role of Entertainment Officer (EO). This suited me as it could be a very useful way of getting alongside the sailors. I had some experience of shipboard entertainment from my frigate squadron days but this was a bigger ship and, as such, it was wise to seek out those who had done it before. Consequently, that evening I went down to No 1 Chief's Mess, who were to become my very best friends, and talked to them about the kind of entertainment that could be provided.

The next day I put a note on Daily Orders asking for volunteers for a Welfare and Entertainment committee and we selected people drawn from all parts of the ships. The entertainment started a few days later on the Saturday afternoon with a tug-of-war on the flight deck and although I can't remember which mess won they were awarded a trophy the Chief Steward found in his store. It was competed for throughout the deployment.

One of the great things about a bigger ship is that it had a TV studio and as EO, I had free and open access to this media. It enabled me to record things like 'Thought for the Day' and we were able to have a televised ship's company quiz.

It was decided that Thursday night would be the ship's quiz night when all messes would compete, including the

Wardroom. There would be prizes, so the interest was high. On one occasion I organized a 'Trivial Pursuit' evening for the messes in the midst of which we had a signal to divert to look for a Russian submarine which was reported to be on fire southeast of Bermuda, so we paused the quiz, turned into the sea and headed for her location.

The following day was Sunday and church was rigged in the junior ratings dining hall and even though a Replenishment At Sea (RAS) had been organized for 0930, so it seemed likely that church would be affected. It was standing room only, with about 50 attending and 31 Communicants. We had an excellent service even though we were moving at 22 knots to intercept the Russian sub. Keeping upright was a challenge but things sliding about did not spoil the service and the band were very good, their practicing was bearing fruit! *Diomede* and *Apollo*, both Leander class frigates who also had officer cadets and apprentices on board, were in company with us. The following day we had news that the Russian submarine had sunk so we reverted to our original course heading for Trinidad.

Chapter Ten

O Islands in the Sun

We arrived in Port of Spain on 10 October. First impressions were that it was a fairly dreary place. The ubiquitous cocktail party held on first night was hard work but I met the Dean of Trinidad Cathedral. Usually we would attend a service ashore and meet local congregations but the High Commission had not been in touch with the church authorities so nothing had been arranged.

During our visit we were invited to use the swimming pool and gym at the Hilton Hotel. It was a lovely pool and the other facilities were excellent too. The weather was grim so it was a welcome change to be able to get off the ship and enjoy different surroundings.

The following Sunday church was held on the fo'cstle at 1000. The Captain was keen that we should have it on the upper deck, so awnings were rigged but it wasn't the most successful of services. It had to be Morning Prayer rather than Holy Communion, as no one could move around because of the risk that civilian guests might trip and fall.

The following afternoon I made a courtesy call upon the Bishop of Trinidad. His house was set in wonderful grounds and as I waited for the front door to be opened, a hummingbird, with such beautiful plumage flew into some foliage near the front door. What a contrast to the gloomy weather. I was eventually admitted and enjoyed talking to the Bishop, who was both courteous and welcoming.

After our meeting, I had no sooner left the Bishop's house when the heavens opened and the rain hammered down. I sheltered under a shop awning with a lot of other people, and we watched the water slowly creeping up the pavement towards us. Then, just as suddenly as it had started, the downpour stopped and I was able to pick my way through the flooded streets back to the ship. We sailed the following morning and were joined by four Trinidadian midshipman, whom I was delighted to host during their short stay on board.

Ceremonial Divisions were held, another factor of training, particularly since we had the Admiral on board. It was incredibly hot and very uncomfortable but in the afternoon we had a 'banyan'. For the uninitiated a 'banyan' is a sort of Naval picnic, held on an island close to the ship.

We returned to Trinidad and the Admiral departed the ship. The following day was Saturday and as soon as leave was piped, a number of us had a 'round island tour' by minibus. The driver knew his stuff and provided an extremely informative talk about the island as we went along. It was, however, very, very hot and humid inside the minibus so we were asked if we would like a drink of cold water. We all said, 'Yes Please', assuming there was a café nearby with refrigerated bottled water. To our surprise the driver stopped the bus alongside a low building built on stilts. Once stopped the driver called out and from underneath the house we could see a man rising from a plank of wood. He approached the minibus and when the driver said we wanted cold drinks, he picked up a machete, shinned up a palm tree and chopped down half a dozen coconuts. He then sliced the tops off and gave them to us. The coconut water inside was ice cold. It was extraordinary but absolutely delicious. The driver told us what the payment would be and we duly gave the man his money. He slowly walked back under the house and got back onto the plank and we continued on our tour.

We sailed the following day at 0900. It was unusual to sail on a Sunday but as soon as we had secured, church was held at 1000 on the flight deck which was a big mistake. I had grave misgivings but the Captain insisted. When I was thinking of joining the Navy some years before, I remember talking to a former chaplain called Gwyndaf Hughes who was very kind and related to me this story.

When he was chaplain on board the old *Ark Royal*, he had held a service of Holy Communion on the quarter deck which had openings on three sides. Gwyndaf was using a throat microphone so that the service could be broadcast to the entire ship's company whether they came to church or not. He had just finished the Prayer of

Consecration when the wind shifted and the stern of this mighty vessel slid into a trough and a gust of wind blew the chalice over, containing the consecrated wine and water. Gwyndaf said, 'There was nothing I could do about it but instinctively I said, "Oh shit", forgetting that I had the throat mic on and my expletive boomed throughout the ship, which caused great amusement for everyone else but great embarrassment to me. So never celebrate on the upper deck if you can avoid it.'

I was determined that that wouldn't happen to me but here I was, about to celebrate on the upper deck. Remembering what Gwyndaf had said, I asked if we could have the hangar door raised and a makeshift altar set up inside the hangar with the congregation and the band seated on the flight deck facing the hangar. Although it was incredibly hot it was also very windy so much so that my notes and service booklets and wafers were in serious danger of being blown all over the place. It was an exercise that I hope wouldn't be repeated.

Jamaica

We arrived at Kingston, Jamaica early on the morning of Friday 24 October. The ship had to be made ready for the usual cocktail party scheduled for that evening and although it was hard work it was always recognized that for those who came to these events it was a completely new experience, held in the most unusual surroundings.

In the afternoon it had been arranged, via the

Consulate, that a party from the ship would visit a local primary school and redecorate it. Whenever ships of the Royal Navy visit foreign ports, the ships' companies always try to carry out some practical work to help a local charity or organization. In this case, the local primary school was in need of redecorating and it would help the local School Board whose finances did not allow for the work. The arrangement was that the school board paid for the paint and we provided the labour. So, a goodly crowd comprising some apprentices, officers under training, members of the ship's company, one of the regulators and me, went to the school by minibus with all our equipment.

The school was very poor, it had a packed earth floor and was in desperate need of attention, so the first thing we had to do was to get all the desks and the furniture out and stacked to one side. The school was really just one big room with some storage rooms and the teacher's office to one side. The teacher was a delight and although she wanted to help but we wouldn't let her do any lifting or carrying. We dragged all the furniture out and I always remember there being one large wooden trunk with a lid. 'What's in the box?' I asked. 'I think its books,' she said and it was. We were outside in the sunshine when we lifted the lid and hundreds upon hundreds of cockroaches poured out of the box, it was exactly like something out of a horror film, the cockroaches scattering all over the place.

During the lunch break some of the children came to

watch us. Our packed lunches included apples. We were mystified by the fact that the children were just staring at us. I said to the teacher, 'Do you not have any apples?' 'Can't get them,' she replied, 'they don't grow on the islands and they're very expensive'. So I said to the PO Regulator, 'Why don't we jump in the bus, go back to the ship. I'll talk to the Supply Officer and see if we can help?' So that's what we did and when we returned with a box of apples you would swear those children had been given Christmas presents early, each of them getting an apple!

We finished the work and in addition we put up a swing and a seesaw, paid for out of the ship's Welfare Fund. It was a joy to see the look on their faces. They had a 'new' classroom and everyone was delighted. Our work had been worthwhile and it was good PR for the ship and the Royal Navy.

Caribbean Idyll

The following morning we sailed at 0800 and stooged around Jamaica for a little while before heading for Port Canaveral. There was a certain amount of excitement on the part of the cadets and apprentices at the prospect of visiting the USA and everyone was looking forward to visiting Florida.

We arrived in Port Canaveral early on the Thursday afternoon and we were able to have the usual 'postcard run' and prepare for the cocktail party.

Next day, just before we sailed for Nassau in the

Bahamas, a film company appeared. The Chaplain of the Fleet had obtained funds so that a film about chaplains in the Royal Navy could be produced as a recruiting aid. The sea-going part of it was down to me. This film company first appeared in St Ann's on the day that we celebrated the 200th anniversary of the church. I had been cross with them because of the noise they were making prior to the start of the service. I hadn't got off to the best of starts with the producer and guess what, he was sharing my cabin! After a slight hesitation we soon got on like a house on fire. They would be with us for the next two weeks, filming all aspects of our life on board. The film company were given a free rein to film what they wished. I believe they had a double role, which was to film me and also the officers under training, so there were many occasions when they were able to film both at the same time.

For example, there was a contrived scene with me talking to a group of officer cadets about their journals; on Remembrance Sunday there was a celebration of Holy Communion at 0800 in the Admiral's cabin and then at 1030 there was the Service of Remembrance on the flight deck, all of which they filmed.

We arrived at Nassau the following morning and again the usual routine of rigging awnings and preparations for the cocktail party got under way. This cocktail party was the best yet. The way it worked was a list of guests would be pinned up in the wardroom and officers would put their names alongside those whom they considered the most interesting. I saw a 'Mr and Mrs Stan Matthews' on the list and as nobody had put their name alongside, so I wrote mine.

When the guests arrived the 'hookers' as they were called (officers under training who had been allocated this duty) met the guests and led them to the host officer. Mr and Mrs Matthews turned out to be Sir Stanley and Lady Matthews, probably one of the greatest England footballers of all time. An awful lot of officers tried to 'muscle in' but to no avail. 'Call me Stan,' he said, 'and this is Betty'. We had a lovely evening and I invited them down to the Wardroom for a drink afterwards. He asked if I had a son who played football, when I said that I did, Stan wrote on the back of his invitation card 'To my little pal John. Best wishes, Sir Stan'. John still has it, as I framed it for him. Sir Stanley was in the Bahamas coaching local youngsters.

Next morning a party made up of all sections of the ship was due to go to a children's hospital in the town. This was a charitable organisation and we were to organise a barbecue. I was delayed because one of the leading writers had gone AWOL He had disappeared overnight and I was summoned to find him. I said I would try but in the middle of Nassau, the capital city, I would need to be a clairvoyant.

I was throwing up 'arrow prayers' left right and centre as I walked through Nassau and lo and behold sitting at a table at a cafe on the seafront was Leading Writer O'Hare. He was a very bright and intelligent man and it transpired that he had had a relationship with a woman and considered himself to be engaged. This woman had two children, was a divorcee and had moved into his house. As soon as we'd sailed, she cleaned out his bank account and then began proceedings to take the house from him. He was in utter despair and he decided that he was going to take his own life. I said, 'Let's have another coffee and talk about it so I have the facts clear in my head and then this is what I propose…' He came back with me and when I talked with his Divisional Officer no charges were to be brought. I then contacted Naval Personal Family Services (NPFS), the Navy's social workers and explained the predicament. They, in turn, contacted the Naval legal people and, it transpired that though he couldn't get his money back, proceedings were begun to have her evicted. It didn't stop him from being heartbroken but he wasn't the first sailor to be taken in by a woman and he won't be the last.

I did get to the hospital in time to help with the barbecue and the games and it was good to see that the children had enjoyed the occasion.

Bermuda

We slipped at 1000 from Nassau heading for Bermuda. We had been pretty lucky with the weather up to now because the 'Windies' can be very stormy at certain times of the year but our luck was about to run out: t
the weather deteriorated rapidly. During the night the

it worsened. One of the few times when I had to strap myself into my bunk, which was part of a unit containing a desk and lots of drawers. You have to remember that *Fife* was quite an elderly lady by this time and my cabin had been knocked around for quite some time with the result that the drawer catches didn't work and as I lay in my bunk all I could do was to listen to the chaos around me – the drawers 'exploding' on the deck with the contents strewn everywhere.

There wasn't much sleep to be had that night and in the morning the first task I had to do was to pick up all my clothes and belongings and put them back in the drawers, replace the drawers and try somehow to wedge them into place. So I went to see the 'chippy' (ship's carpenter) and had some little wedges made that I could push in to the tops of the drawers to stop them sliding out.

The movement of the ship made it difficult to move around, to write or to mark and although at times I felt queasy I still managed to eat and to stay on my feet, whereas lots of the ship's company were in their bunks feeling very ill.

Despite the heavy weather we arrived at Ireland Island in Bermuda in the forenoon. Before the Second World War, Ireland Island was the home of the Royal Navy's North America Squadron when the Royal Navy was much, much bigger. The names of some of those ships had been painted on the dockyard walls showing the long link that Bermuda had with the Royal Navy. Inside the reef the sea was much calmer and the weather improved slightly and we were able to hold the cocktail party in the evening.

It's quite interesting to observe a change in attitude regarding Sunday church services, which came the following day, because the Bishop of Bermuda was coming on board to celebrate Holy Communion in the Wardroom. Not the ideal place for the service but the weather put the fo'castle and the flight deck out of bounds and the timing prevented the junior rates dining hall being used. I wanted to use one of the other ships *Apollo* or *Diomede* but the Captain wouldn't hear of it. *Fife* was the Dartmouth Training Ship and it would be in his ship that any kind of celebration like this would take place. I thought that it was a pity the same attitude wasn't shown when we were in other ports, when I was told, 'It's a quiet Sunday, you can't have church'. It's amazing what a bishop's mitre can do! Anyway, it was a good service, the bishop celebrated and preached and he was very good chatting to the sailors over coffee before he went off to another function.

We sailed from Bermuda the following day. The weather had improved, though a long slow swell caused the ship to roll quite a bit.

During the crossing from Bermuda to the Azores I had the opportunity of talking to the apprentices and the young officers on the role of the Chaplain in the Royal Navy. I had been with them for some weeks and worked alongside many of them and spoken to most of them but nevertheless they were not really churchgoers. They were typical products of the British society, so it was an opportunity to explain why the Church is involved with the Royal Navy, with its similar traditions and history. It was also an opportunity to make a statement about the Christian Faith. One of the problems of chaplaincy work is that 'you can cast your bread upon the water' but you never know if anybody nibbles.

We arrived back in Pompey and learned that *Fife* would be 'paying off' at the end of the summer cruise the following year. So she had just something like 8 months left of her commission. There was a ship's Welfare Committee meeting a few days later when the Supply Officer pointed out that if we did not spend the money in the Welfare Fund it would, on de-commissioning, be paid into the Fleet Canteen Fund to be spent by others. I said, 'If you don't want to lose it, spend it'. They said, 'On what?' so the Entertainment Committee and I came up with the idea that we would have a ship's company dance which would be free to all members of the ship's company and their partners. It would take place in the summer of the following year on our return from the United States but the planning needed to start immediately. In addition we decided to have a ship's company raffle.

As we would soon be going on our next cruise to the Mediterranean we needed to get the basics sorted out within the next few weeks.

Since *Fife* was technically within the Portsmouth area,

she came under Portsmouth City Council when conforming to civic by-laws. In other words, we had to have a license to sell raffle tickets. So as the Entertainment Officer I talked to the relevant person in the Civic Offices and the whole thing was registered in my name. We had a meeting to decide on suitable prizes and the first prize would have to be something substantial. One of our number had a friend who had been in the Navy but and who then had a car dealership. Having spoken to him we found that he was prepared to sell us a brand new Volvo at trade price, around £5,000, so the first thing we had to do was to sell £5,000 worth of raffle tickets. It was my job to order thousands of raffle tickets and to book a venue for the ship's company dance before we left for the next deployment.

It might be worthwhile stating at this point that the reason that we went to interesting places was not because their Lordships had a sudden rush of blood to the head, but to 'follow the sun'; because if you want to teach someone navigation it is better to do it in fine, sunny weather rather than in screaming gales. So, by and large, the destinations of the Dartmouth Training Squadron or in this case, the Dartmouth Training Ship, was to areas of the world and at the times of the year when the weather would be more likely to be good. After the usual pre-Christmas celebrations, leave commenced on 19 December and ended on 6 January 1987 and my New Year began with an appointment in London to see the Chaplain of the Fleet. In the course of the interview I was told that once *Fife* 'paid off', I was to join the 6th Frigate Squadron.

Chapter Eleven

If You Sail the Mediterranean You Must Call and See the Pope!

We sailed for our Spring Deployment to the Mediterranean on the 12 January. We were in company with HMS *Intrepid*, also acting Dartmouth Training Ship, as she also had Officers under Training and Apprentices on board. *Intrepid*'s chaplain was my old 'chum' Godfrey Hilliard, so our paths had crossed again. With the end of each 'term' there came a change in the officer cadets and apprentices who, having spent 2-3 months on-board, went off to continue their courses elsewhere. This resulted in a complete change of faces, including some of the instructors. One of the instructors who came on board as a divisional officer was one Michael Satchwell, who became my very best friend on board and our friendship continued for many years. I really valued his company as there were few on board who wanted to go ashore with the vicar!

Over the next couple of days the ship underwent deck landings and other tests in readiness for the 'Thursday War' at Portland. This weekly occurrence involved a number of ships whose capabilities were tested by the Portland staff in all aspects of security and safety, as well as the ability to fight. On completion of the 'Thursday War', we left Portland and arrived in Brest, the Naval Base on the northwest coast of France, for a 'goodwill' visit. However, memory tells me that there wasn't a great deal of goodwill, in fact the reaction of the civilians we met was quite frosty, except for the base chaplain.

Brest is a very large naval base and the senior chaplain was a man called Louis le Stat, who was, of course, Roman Catholic. He was an exceptionally nice man, very kind to me and, indeed, entertained a number of us in his home where he and I had discussions about the differences between the Roman Catholic and Anglican churches. He was a very erudite and hospitable man whom I remember with deep gratitude.

Preparations for the paying off of the ship were moving ahead and the ship's noticeboard on the 'Great Glen' had been cleared. To encourage the sale of raffle tickets I had an enlarged photograph of the prize car. When we had enough money for a wheel then I would cut out the wheel from the photograph and stick it on the board and gradually bit-by-bit the picture of the car grew depending on the number of tickets sold. Once the target figure was raised then the dealer was contacted and the car purchased. We began to look at other prizes but we decided we couldn't do that until we got back to Portsmouth. All of this was not what I'd been trained to do but it did put me alongside sailors and it did give me an opportunity to show the church being involved in the day-to-day running of the ship. It was also very good training for me as years later fundraising became a central part of my life!

Earlier I mentioned the day-to-day routines which, for me, included saying the Daily Offices (Morning and Evening Prayer), teaching English for NAMET and 'O'Level.

We also had a Bible Study group. Quite a number of the young officer cadets and apprentices were from a Christian background, so about 15 would gather to study the Bible of an evening, once or twice a week, ending with a short service of Compline. I found those times very meaningful. They counterbalanced some of the more secular things that I was involved in, like selling raffle tickets. I'd like to think that their Christian faith was enhanced and challenged by the prayers and discussions that we held in what was, after all, very different surroundings from the ones that any of us would be used to when it comes to Bible study or prayer groups.

We were heading south towards Funchal, the capital of Madeira. The weather was awful and we were heading into heavier weather, so the ship was taking a bit of a pounding. We arrived in Funchal on Saturday 24 January, although the approach was difficult. We were to berth on the inside of the mole (jetty) but because *Fife* was such a big ship and high out of the water, the wind kept trying to push us off. We were therefore secured by hurricane hawsers, although but that didn't really stop the ship from bouncing around inside the harbour. Indeed, there were people who felt seasick during the cocktail party because the ship was rolling back and forth. For us it was just a gentle motion but those who were not used to ships found it very uncomfortable.

During the cocktail party the First Lieutenant had to leave because we had severed a hurricane hawser which had to be replaced, otherwise we could have swung across the harbour and become aground. One of the guests was the Rev'd Arthur Walters, a former Parachute Regiment chaplain serving in the Diocese of Europe as chaplain to the Anglican congregation in Funchal. The Bishop of Fulham and Gibraltar also attended because there was to be a Confirmation in the church the following evening. Consequently, the next day, Third Sunday after Epiphany we attended the English church in Funchal. The Bishop preached and the place was packed, with a goodly number from the ship being a part of this large congregation. I did not know it then but I was to worship in that church on a number of occasions in the future.

We sailed on the Wednesday into very heavy weather and that night the ship was rolling so severely, very little sleep was had by anyone. I again strapped myself into my bunk but my cabin was not littered with drawers and papers because the wedges worked perfectly. I dreaded to think what conditions were like in *Intrepid* because she would roll in a heavy dew! In actual fact, *Intrepid* sustained damage to her rudder so we had to put into Gibraltar for repairs, which meant an unexpected run ashore. We sailed the following morning (Saturday) and the weather had improved considerably so much so, that we were able to hold a 100 x 1 mile relay on board in aid of charity. I did my 1-mile going round and round the upper deck.

Our next port of call was Livorno, the Italian version of Dartmouth and the home of their Naval College. *Fife* went to Livorno whilst *Intrepid* put into Naples. We were due in on Thursday 5 February but on Tuesday afternoon, I was called to the Main Communications Office (MCO) to take a shore to ship phone call. 'Who on earth could be calling me?' I wondered. It turned out to be Her Majesty's Ambassador to the Holy See. He asked if we would like to meet the Pope? Now, every Thursday morning in St Peter's Square the public gather for a Papal Blessing, so given the distance involved and our limited time in Italy I didn't think anybody would be interested. I said, 'Your Excellency, are we talking about the usual Thursday gathering?' 'No,' he said, 'this is a private audience in the Papal apartments.' I said, 'I'm sure that we would be very interested in that'. He informed me that whilst we would be travelling down from Livorno people from *Intrepid* would be coming up from Naples. The stipulation was that we would wear uniform. After a moment to consider all the implications, I made a 'pipe' to the ship's company telling them that we had received this invitation and if anyone would be interested in visiting Rome and the Pope, please to let me know as soon as possible because the spaces would be limited.

Within ten minutes a lot of people contacted me, many of whom were not Roman Catholics but it was surprising the number of Romans who suddenly appeared when the Pope was mentioned! With the help of the Italian liason officer a coach was hired very quickly.

I arranged with the galley that an early breakfast could be served at 0530 as the coach was departing for Rome at 0630. We arrived at about 1130 and went straight to the Basilica of St Peter and St Paul. The coach driver knew exactly where we were going and took us close to the entrance. The entrance to the Papal apartments is on the right of the colonnade that runs across the front of the basilica and is guarded by a member of the Carabinieri. Our liaison officer went to speak to him and eventually members of the Swiss Guard, the Pope's personal guard, came down to escort us to the Papal apartments.

We assembled in this huge room with wonderful murals around the upper part of the walls. There was a raised dais at one end with a microphone on a stand. We were to remain standing throughout the audience. Eventually an attendant informed us that the Pope would either sit on the throne and speak to us from there in which case, on completion of his greeting, we would gather around him for photographs or he would go to the microphone, speak to us standing on his feet and on completion come down among us. This is what he did and after his brief speech and Blessing he stepped off the podium and came down to us.

I represented HMS *Fife* and, as the senior ship, I stepped forward and presented him with the ship's badge on behalf of the Captain and the ship's company. Godfrey Hilliard did the same for *Intrepid*. I then escorted His Holiness through our people and when he stopped to chat with someone I introduced them. The first person he came to was a young steward whose name was John Cosmac, he was from Liverpool. The Holy Father said to him 'Good morning, how are you?' Cosmac couldn't find his tongue and was mumbling so I tapped him on the head and said, 'Answer the Holy Father,' the Pope looked at me and said, 'I see the Royal Navy has not lost its sense of discipline.' I laughed and said, 'Holy Father this young man's grandfather came from your hometown.' The Pope looked at Cosmac and said, 'So, your grandfather was with the Free Polish forces in the war?' Cosmac replied, 'Yes Holy Father,' they then chatted briefly. Then the Pope said to him, 'Please take to your grandfather and your family my Papal blessing and my deep affection for them.'

We moved on and a number of other people from *Fife* were introduced to the Pope and I then passed the Pope on to Godfrey to be introduced to their people. We were closely shadowed by members of the Curia so we didn't have long with him. He eventually took his leave of us, we thanked him profusely and there was a massive round of applause as he left the audience chamber.

We re-embarked in the coaches for a very brief tour of central Rome and some of the sites and then drove back to Livorno and Naples respectively. A round trip of 700 km for just 4 hours in Rome but it was worth it. A footnote to this visit was that on our return to Portsmouth, families came to welcome the ship home and I met Cosmac's family including his grandfather who was in tears and went down on one knee and grabbed my hand and kissed it in gratitude for what I had done! I was so embarrassed, I quickly helped him to his feet and assured him that I had done nothing. Apparently the family's standing within the Polish community in Liverpool had rocketed and, according to him, it was all down to me. Nice to have fans!

At the cocktail party the previous evening one of the guests was the Bishop of Leghorn. Livorno is in the District of Leghorn. The Bishop and I talked at length and he told me that he was going to be away on Sunday afternoon but if I wanted to borrow his car and driver I would be most welcome to do so. I was only too pleased to accept his kind offer so following church in the Junior Ratings Dining Hall the next day I, and a few of the liaison officers who were still on board, climbed into the car and off we set.

We went to Pisa with its famous 'Leaning Tower', just how much it leans becomes more apparent when you try to climb up the inside. On the driver's recommendation, we went to the village of Piero de Grada, and I am so glad we did. It's about 10 miles from Pisa. He took us to the little village church, which initially seemed to be nothing special, but on inspection it was quite amazing. Around the upper walls there were magnificent murals dating from the 11th century. At the back of the church, an excavation was taking place which revealed a pathway showing that a church had been on that site since the first century. Local legend has it that the people of the Leghorn District worked on the salt marshes which were prevalent all along the coast. Salt was a hugely important part of the economy of Ancient Rome and its Empire, so they were very well-to-do people and they were also Christians. When St Peter went to Italy he did not go directly to Rome but to Leghorn and to Piero de Grada. It is said that he remained with them for some time before setting off for Rome and his martyrdom.

Standing at the back of that church, looking at this cobbled pathway, I wondered whether St. Peter himself had worshipped on that site because a church would have stood there at that time. We'll never know but there had been Mass that morning and the smell of incense still hung in the air. That continuity of faith meant more to me than all the treasures of the Basilica of St. Peter's and Paul. This simple little village parish church had links with the origins of the Faith. I was deeply moved by the whole experience and thanked the driver for taking me there. I felt I had seen one of the great treasures of Italy.

Photographs

Part of St Anne's choir

St Anne's 200th

Action Church
HMS Invincible

Receiving my Second Commission from
The Chaplain of the Fleet

Bishop Timothy

A light jack stay transfer

Our visit to the Vatican

The Pope and I

Dead Sea
I tried walking but failed

Another good deed

Dedicating Royal Marine HQ

Entering the St Lawrence Seaway

The school we worked on

Upper deck BBQ

HMS St David showing the A bracket

HMS Fife

Alamein
Sailors past and present

Cemetary at El Alamain
one small section

A view of Jerusalem

Guess where

Sea Harrier shadowing a Russian 'Bear D'.

Stan Matthews' greeting

HMS Plymouth

HMS Invincible 3

10th Sept '91

Invincible - busy time!

School visit to Swansea

Chapter Twelve

Istanbul and the Greek Islands

We sailed the following morning for Istanbul. Part of our voyage would take us through the extraordinary Corinth Canal. This is an amazing piece of engineering. Construction began in 1881. Before that, people crossed this narrow neck of land on a 'boat rail', which were small boats fitted onto wheeled trolleys pulled by horses. Creating a canal through this neck of land enabling vessels to sail through greatly reduced the trading time. The Canal has a depth of 8m or 27 feet and its length is just about 4 miles. *Fife* could just about fit through it but *Intrepid* could not.

Having sailed from Livorno we transited the Tyrrhenian Sea, went around Sicily, sailed north of Malta and headed for Corinth. We transited this extraordinary canal with the walls rising sheer above us and on a bridge crossing the canal we could see school children waving down at us from far above. It was a tight squeeze and the buffers party were back and forth with baulks of timber hanging over the ships side acting as fenders, in case we bumped the walls. It was a great photo opportunity and everyone enjoyed the experience.

We emerged unscathed into the Aegean Sea and made

our way through the Cyclades Islands, up to Istanbul where we arrived on Friday 13 February in the forenoon.

We anchored in the 'Golden Horn', a stretch of water between Europe and Asia. I had been fortunate enough to visit Istanbul some years before whilst on board HMS *Berwick* and the excitement was still the same. It's amazing and the smell and sounds of this great city are always intriguing. *Intrepid* was moored near us and the cocktail party was to take place there.

Istanbul was noisy, crowded, dirty, choked with traffic and heavily polluted but it is still one of the most exciting cities on the planet and I loved it. The Grand Bazaar was one of its particular glories and the Spice Market was equally beguiling. We sailed early in the afternoon after a most exciting visit.

Our next destination was Thessalonica but before that, we made diversion to the Holy Island of Athos. Legend has it that the Virgin Mary, the Mother of our Lord, known in the Greek Orthodox Church as the Theotokos, which is, 'God Bearer' or 'Mother of God' took passage in a ship bound for Cyprus but was blown off course and landed at Mount Athos. Forever after it has been known as the Holy Island. It is home to a number of monasteries from the different branches of the Orthodox Christian Faith: Greek Orthodox, Russian Orthodox, Romanian Orthodox. No female is allowed on the island and no child either, which can be a problem for visiting cruise liners. In fact, whilst we were there a cruise liner came in and moored at the jetty but the ladies who came ashore had to stay in the customs post, they were not allowed to go any further.

We, on the other hand, were allowed to go inland and were welcomed by monks of the Greek monastery with great courtesy and with refreshments. We were shown around by one of the young monks who spoke halting English. In the chapels there were icons of the Blessed Virgin and other saints. When people came to visit, perhaps on pilgrimage, they would present their prayers and then leave a gift near the icons. These gifts could be anything, money, watches, anything that mattered to them.

After a very short visit we continued on to Thessalonica, arriving on Friday 20 February. Following the usual cocktail party I received a request to take an evening service in the local Greek Orthodox church for ex patriots, as they were allowed to use the church on Sunday evenings. I readily agreed and reciprocated by inviting them to a celebration of Holy Communion at 0800 on board.

Later, on a beautiful evening, I and others strolled along to the church. The local expatriates had asked if the band would come and play at the service, which they readily agreed to do. We held a traditional Evensong and, to my great amusement, a number of local Greeks gathered at the back of the church, puzzled by the music. The Orthodox tradition does not have choirs or organs or bands, so when people heard the band playing in the church they just wandered in to find out what was going on. It seemed to me that there were more people standing at the back of the church than were in the congregation. I was grateful to the priest for allowing us the use of the church.

We sailed on the Monday morning heading for home but we put into Gibraltar which, as always, was a delight. The sailors availed themselves of Main Street, the 'Angry Friar' and the other establishments that they so enjoyed. We arrived back in Portsmouth on the morning of Thursday 5 March.

Chapter Thirteen

The Kingdom of Fife and the Pool of London

Our time in Portsmouth was limited because we were due to sail for Dundee on 11 March. The officers under training disembarked and returned to Dartmouth so the ship felt quite empty when we sailed to visit the 'Kingdom of Fife'. With the ship bearing this ancient name it was felt that a final goodwill visit would be the right thing to do.

We arrived in Dundee on Thursday and there was the usual cocktail party, when local people were entertained on board and then hospitality was extended to us by various people, to include an allocation of tickets to watch the match between Dundee and Dundee United. .We sailed from Dundee on the Tuesday and arrived in the Pool of London on Wednesday 18 March. The passage up the Thames was really impressive, being under the control of a river pilot, and we berthed outboard of HMS *Belfast*. A number of invitations came our way, one of which was a tour of Tower Bridge, including the inner workings of the Bridge. Whilst in the control room, a ship passed downstream, so we witnessed the raising of the bascules and how that mechanism worked. It is a brilliant piece of engineering.

It was a hugely enjoyable visit and were treated with great courtesy by the Bridge watch keepers.

Another of the Pool of London highlights was that we were to embark 'Sons at Sea.' This is a scheme that was held in the Navy at that time, when the sons of serving personnel could, where applicable, join the ships in which their fathers served and have a few days at sea. There was an age limit and, though John was a little younger than usual, it was agreed that he could join us, as he would share my cabin since I had double bunk space. We sailed down the Thames and out into the English Channel, our destination being Portland where we were to carry out deck landing training. On arrival the boys disembarked and were put into a coach for Portsmouth.

Upon my return to Portsmouth I had to see the Chaplain of the Fleet regarding leaving *Fife* at the end of the next deployment and joining the 6th Frigate Squadron. There was also other administrative tasks to complete both in relation to the paying off dance and charities the sailors supported while at sea but, on 21 April, we sailed for our summer deployment. We had already embarked 78 Officers under training from Dartmouth and 34 Engineering apprentices for sea training. This one was an odd deployment, I say 'odd' because the places that we were to visit were not the usual ports of call and I don't think it's ever happened since because we were bound for The Great Lakes. It was to be an extensive voyage with a lot of port visits, all of which would be to promote Great Britain. *Fife* would be accompanied by HM Ships *Euryalus*, *Apollo* and *Juno*. There would be approximately 1000 sailors in all. It was a major deployment so it was important that we got it right.

Chapter Fourteen

The Great Lakes and the Windy City

We entered the St. Lawrence River leading into the Seaway, which is 370 miles in length. This is a series of canals and locks enabling large ships to enter the Great Lakes. Work on the locks began before 1871 and gradually more locks and canals were constructed until the completed. Seaway was opened in 1959 by Queen Elizabeth, as Queen of Canada, and President Eisenhower, President of the United States. When we reached Chicago on the banks of Lake Michigan we were 182 metres above sea level. The Seaway is another superb engineering feat, just like the Panama Canal and the Suez Canal, though constructed over a period of time. It has had a great economic impact on the mid-West of the United States and Canada alike.

Our first destination was Quebec, a very nice city and very friendly people but in all the ports we visited the pattern was largely the same: we would arrive on a Friday, there would be a cocktail party arranged by the consulate and we would sail on the Monday.

Our next destination was Montreal followed by Toronto, which was special for me because my brother Colin and family lived about 60 miles outside the city and they were able to attend the cocktail party. Afterward, I was granted a few days leave to spend with them. From there we moved on to Chicago, the pinnacle of the deployment.

Chicago is an amazing city but had a great record for violence. It's not just a case of the 'St. Valentine's Day Massacre'. We were told that the United States Navy had one ship's visit a year and there was always at least one murder. As a result, the Chicago police were petrified at the prospect of 1000 British sailors being let loose in the city. To prevent any problems, the Chief of Police came out to the ship, a couple of days prior to our arrival and talked to the officers and liaison team. His advice on the do's and don'ts was passed on to the ship's company via TV and radio and Daily Orders. I have always found Americans to be amazingly friendly, generous and hospitable people but they are ferociously patriotic. Though we share a similar language, it is a foreign country and they have their own way of doing things and we needed to be aware of that.

We arrived in Chicago on Thursday 21 May. The following evening we had the ubiquitous cocktail party, however the pattern of the visit changed because that night, Petty Officer George Small and three of his 'oppos' went ashore for a few beers and a look around. On_their way back to the ship, in the time honoured British fashion, they had asked directions from a policeman. They approached a parked police car, tapped on the window and said, 'Excuse me constable, can you direct us to our ship, please?'

What we didn't know was that the Chicago Police Force had been told to handle us with kid gloves and to be as helpful as possible, so the policeman got out of the car and said to George, 'Jump in the car and we will give you a lift'. 'Am I being arrested?' said George, 'No' said the cop, 'just get in the car!' So George and his chums got in the car and were whisked back to the ship. When they arrived at the pier George invited the policeman and his companion to 4 Mess for a drink. So they went down to the Mess with their guns! A massive 'No, no'.

The following morning, when the commander found out that there had been guns on board, he hit the roof (or rather the deck head!) and instructions were given to the entire ship's company that nobody was to come on board carrying weapons. This was to prove a little bit embarrassing when a few days later the Mayor of Chicago came on board for a presentation and his entourage included bodyguards, who were armed.

It made no difference, they too had to leave their guns with the duty watch on the gangway when they arrived and collect them when they left. But George Small's introduction to the Chicago Police broadened out because the police, if they saw our sailors waiting or wandering about, would always ask if they wanted a lift and frequently gave tours of the city. I think they quite enjoyed it all which is more than can be said of the taxi companies!

On the Sunday I had been invited to preach at St.

James' Cathedral and was delighted to accept. It was interesting to see the difference between how the Episcopal Church in America was run compared to the Church of England at the time; there were five or six clergy on the staff, including the Dean, one of them was a Welshman, who asked me a great deal about things at home; they weren't all paid by the cathedral authorities, some being self-financing; there was no such thing as the Church Commissioners, each congregation being financially independent; and the choir was professional. I preached at the main Eucharist and it was a welcome change to have such a large congregation in front of me. Incidentally, the view from the top of the Sears building was amazing.

Although the visit was almost a week it seemed much longer and we had a wonderful reception wherever we went and were treated with great hospitality and kindness. As we were due to sail that forenoon the two detectives who had been our constant companions came down to see us off in an ordinary police car and as a joke somebody said, 'Wouldn't it be great if we could mark our visit with a memento of the Police Department since they had done so much for us?' One of our friends promptly unbolted the siren and lights from the top of the car and presented them to us. It was meant as a joke but it showed the generosity and craziness of our visit there. All the preparations and advice beforehand was worthwhile because there was no trouble and no one was killed or injured. The sailors behaved themselves impeccably, as they usually do, and were splendid ambassadors for the Royal Navy and for Great Britain.

Our visit had been, without exception, a great success. Nevertheless, I'll bet there was a huge sigh of relief when we slipped from the jetty. We left Chicago on the 27 May and headed to our next port of call, Milwaukee, arriving two days later. There was just enough time to put the ship in good order before we were preparing for the cocktail party on the Friday night. I have little comment to make on Milwaukee other than it was a nice town, the people were kind and we saw such sites as were there. Unfortunately, we were becoming 'port crazy,' in other words it was one town/city after another and they all began to be a blur.

We left Milwaukee on Monday 1 June and had 3 days transiting the Great Lakes when all 4 ships were able to carry out further navigational training, which is why were there in the first place.

We arrived in Cleveland on 5 June. When WC Field on his deathbed was asked 'How do you feel, Mr Field?' he said allegedly, 'All things considered I'd rather be in Cleveland!' Cleveland did not have the greatest promotion and we were there for 5 days. Yet again it left little impression on me and we left the following Tuesday, heading down the St Lawrence Seaway and into the Atlantic.

We arrived at St John's Newfoundland where we were scheduled to stay for 3 days, during which time we celebrated Trafalgar Night which was a memorable occasion, including fresh lobster caught that morning by the fishermen of St John's.

Leaving St. Johns on Thursday 18 June ,we headed homeward, it was our last Thursday at sea so we had the final of the Thursday Night Quiz, A league table had been set up in the television studio at the beginning of the deployment but many of the messes had fallen behind because they had missed some of the rounds. So beforehand I went round the messes and the workplaces and spoke to the 'killicks' and Mess Presidents some of whom said, 'We are so far behind there is no point,' and I said, 'Yes there is, tonight you'll have a chance to catch up'.

That night the quiz went out on TV for a couple of hours, interspersed with cartoons and augmented at intervals by requests for 'The first mess to bring to the studio a 'Pusser's mattress (or whatever) will get an extra 50 points.' It set the place alight, with groups from different messes trying to get to the studio at the same and 'fighting' to get there first. The quiz nights proved to be very successful.

Chapter Fifteen

Fife's Farewell

As we crossed the Atlantic normal training went on and the normal shipboard activities continued, including navigation training and engineering training for the apprentices.

Our first destination was Dartmouth. The Captain thought it a good idea to drop off the staff and officers under training by going up the River Dart. It would save a long journey by road but it was also a wonderful photo opportunity, because it would be the largest ship ever to enter the River Dart. That was indeed the case but we couldn't turn the ship in the Dart as she was too long, so a tug was sent around from Plymouth to tow us up the Dart backwards! Then we sailed from the Dart in great triumph a few days later. The officers under training and their staff, in gratitude, returned hospitality in the college and the town.

We arrived in Portsmouth on Thursday 25 June and HMS *Fife* became non-operational on 30 June, so the work began to prepare the ship for Disposal. It was then fitting that her life should be celebrated and the Paying off Dance was very timely. The dance itself was a big success, the music was great, the dancing was enthusiastic and the raffle was the pinnacle of the evening.

The first ticket out was drawn by the Captain, the ticket he drew was placed in an envelope which was placed at the top end of the stage where it could be seen by everyone. We wanted to keep the tension going, so gradually bit-by-bit all the prizes that had been gathered in over many weeks were won and then, with a drum roll, that envelope was opened and the winner was named, Marine Engineering Mechanic Johnston.

The dealer who provided us with a car also provided a blouson jacket with 'Volvo' emblazoned across the back. When Johnston come up onto the stage he was presented with the jacket but he was so drunk he thought that's what he'd won. I said to him, 'Where's your ticket?' 'What ticket?' 'The ticket for the car'. 'What car?' 'That bloody car' said one of the committee. 'I thought it was just the jacket,' said Johnston 'No, it's the car now where's the f**** ticket?' 'I don't know,' he said. I asked him, 'When did you last see it?' 'When I went down to the heads.'

'Bloody hell,' said the committee in unison. We really didn't fancy having to draw the whole thing again, so the six members of the committee, including me rushed off to the gent's toilets and began rummaging around on the paper strewn carpet. We went through all the bits of paper that were there and, eventually, we found it. It seemed like an age but it was only a few minutes and with beads of sweat on our foreheads we went back up to the main hall. I called Johnston up to the stage and everybody fell about laughing when we presented him with the ticket for the car.

At lunchtime on the following day the dealer brought the car to the ship, the ship's company lined the side, Johnston wore the jacket and the committee presented him with the keys whilst the photographer from 'Navy News' photographed it all. It had been a long process which came to a successful conclusion and I was mighty relieved that it had.

It was also a fitting end to my chaplaincy on board HMS *Fife*.

Chapter Sixteen

6th Frigate Squadron

On 24 July I assumed the duties as chaplain to the 6th Frigate Squadron. I called upon the Captain of the lead ship *Ariadne,* where all my documents were to be kept. I also saw other relevant people on board, the Master at arms, the PO Steward, the NAAFI manager, so that my details could be logged with them too.

The command was in the process of being changed, with Captain Peter Grindall being relieved by Captain John McAnally.

Ariadne was a ship that I knew well from my time in the 7th Frigate Squadron. At 0800 on Monday I reported to the Captain on board. Captain McAnally was also leader of the Squadron and having 'made my number' with him, I believe we sailed for a very short time (a few days) so that he could get to know the ship and the ship's company. In the afternoon of the second day, there was a knock on my cabin door. It was the Captain's steward who said, 'Captain's complements, sir, but would you be kind enough to have supper with him tonight?' I was delighted to accept and that evening I reported to the Captain's cabin where the table was laid for two people. Captain McAnally was absolutely charming, he was courtesy itself and he and I got on very well. He was a most hospitable host whose acquaintance I was to experience some years later when he came to deliver 'The Immortal Memory' at *HMS Cambria's* Trafalgar Night dinner. By then he had become a Vice Admiral.

The couple of days that we had at sea enabled me to complete my joining routines, as I had done on previous appointments, but this time I was able to sit down and spend time with the Squadron Operations officer working out my programme. It was a curious situation because, as I have said previously, an appointment to a frigate squadron needs to be a minimum of 2 years so that one can spend an adequate amount of time in each ship, getting to know the personnel. My time in this Squadron was going to be less than a year, and given that the ships were scattered, some in refit, others preparing for deployment, others day running, it was going to be difficult to get around them all but I was determined to try to spend as much time as possible in each.

On Monday 10 August, I travelled to Rosyth in Scotland where *HMS Plymouth* was in refit. As she was soon to be recommissioned it was a good opportunity to say 'hello to the ship's company. Also in Rosyth was *HMS Rothesay,* another member of the Squadron in refit, whose Supply Officer I knew very well, Norman Howden whom I had had Confirmed in St Ann's when he and his wife Carol returned from their time in Hong Kong. They were to become very dear friends.

On my return from Rosyth I had just a couple of days

to get my kit from *Ariadne* and into *Juno* as she was due to visit Dieppe in Northern France. This would be the only opportunity that I would have to spend time with the ship's company.

It was a curious feeling to walk along the beach at Dieppe trying to visualize the raid that took place in 1943. It was a disaster, with a tremendous loss of life, but a huge amount of what had been learned was put to good use on D-Day. Nevertheless, for the people who took part in the raid, it was dreadful experience. Memory tells me that ours was a successful visit, the locals were very friendly and we had a few evenings in restaurants and visited local sites. We returned from Dieppe on the 20 August and I had to move my kit again, this time to *HMS Achilles,* before going on leave.

Upon return from leave I attended a first aid course at *HMS Phoenix* which was to last four days. It proved extremely interesting but very demanding. I did reasonably well, and the ships were very happy that I had completed the first aid course, always useful to have another pair of hands that could be put to good use in an emergency. From my perspective it was another way to get alongside people, possibly when they needed help most.

The weekend following my course, *Achilles* was acting as Fleet Contingency Ship which meant being available for any emergency that might occur so when a Russian destroyer began to transit the Channel she was ordered to escort the vessel safely through. I received a phone call on Saturday morning recalling me to the ship as it had to sail at mid-day. I explained that I had to conduct a baptism on board *Juno* next day and as it had been arranged for some time I did not feel that I could let the family down.

It was arranged that I would conduct the baptism and join them at Campeltown on the west coast of Scotland where there is a fueling facility. *Achilles*, having escorted the Russian through the Channel, would carry on around the top of Scotland but would need to top up her tanks before deploying. Which meant that on Monday I had to obtain the necessary warrants to fly to Glasgow and hire a car to drive to Campeltown. There, I joined Achilles as arranged after a very pleasant journey through the Scottish countryside.

Having topped up with fuel, we sailed for a goodwill visit to Lisbon, arriving on the 13 October. The weather since leaving Campbeltown had been particularly heavy. When we arrived at Lisbon it took five approaches before we could get a line onto the jetty. The River Tagus was very rough compared to its usual placid self and we heard reports that commuters had been seasick on the ferries carrying them to work. Lousy start to their day! As soon as we got alongside we discovered that Britain had been hit by what has become known as the 'Great Storm'. We were fortunate to have ducked underneath it, although Britain as a whole had been severely damaged by this cyclone of high winds. The storm was made memorable by the words of the weather forecaster Michael Fish on the BBC, who said 'There isn't going to be a hurricane' but he was wrong and there was, but we missed it.

I have to be honest and say that, though I remember the difficulties of getting alongside, I don't remember much else about that visit. Lisbon is a delightful city which was devastated by an earthquake in the 17th century and rebuilt on classical Roman lines. When you approach from the sea there is the great Monument to the Navigators which is very, very impressive but we sailed from Lisbon on the 19th for Gibraltar.

My friend Godfrey Hilliard was chaplain at Gibraltar and it was good to see him again. But it wasn't all 'beer and skittles' for on the Wednesday we had 'Exercise Awkward' when the ship would be tested to repel land assault. The local resident Army battalion had been tasked to attack the ship at any opportunity and in the most imaginative ways. I was in my cabin marking papers when I heard this commotion outside on the upper deck onto the cabin flat and saw the back of a man coming through the outer screen door with a pistol levelled at the duty watch who were pursuing him. Others too came out of their cabins and as the man moved backwards we pounced on him and took the pistol off him. His target was the Captain but he failed to reach target, though he did get as far as the door to the Captain's cabin. The entire ship's company had to stay on their toes for the rest of the day and night because the exercise wasn't due to finish until 2200 and the battalion could come at us at any time and in any way. It's good training but I have often reflected that the easiest way would be to put the ship in the middle of the harbour where it would become even more difficult for people to get you, but what do I know?

The next morning I was due to take part in the Top of The Rock run, this was to be the second time that I had run the Rock, the first was when I served with 40 Commando. There was to be a third but it was not to come along for several years. I can't remember what time I came in but it was better than my time with the Royal Marines. It is called a 'Run' but given the gradients involved running usually takes place on the bits that are flat.

There were no services on board on the Sunday, as those who wished could go to the cathedral or any other church of their choosing. We sailed the following morning, arriving in Portsmouth on the Friday 30 October when I left *Achilles* and prepared to join *HMS Plymouth* which was due to deploy as Belize Guard Ship.

Chapter Seventeen

A Caribbean Tragedy

I joined *Plymouth* on 15 November in Rosyth and we sailed the following morning to take up the duties as Belize Guard Ship. The deployment had a very interesting programme with the first call being the Azores to take on fuel, from there crossing the Atlantic to Miami, from Miami a visit to Nassau in the Bahamas and from there on to the Dominican Republic.

Next came St. Petersburg's in Florida for Christmas after which the ship was scheduled to visit New Orleans and then on to Vera Cruz before returning home at the end of January. We were in company with an RFA (Royal Fleet Auxiliary) *Grey Rover,* a fleet supply ship and on the Sunday afternoon having taken services in the Junior Ratings dining hall I was taking my ease, when the telephone buzzed. It was the First Lieutenant, Peter Plumb, asking me to go up to the bridge. He told me that a signal had been received requesting me to cross to *Grey Rover* to conduct a service for them. Bang went my afternoon read! I assumed that the helicopter would be launched but that was quickly dispelled, since the cost of launching the helicopter was out of the question, it was to be a sea boat transfer.

From the bridge the sea state did not look too bad, a few white horses around, but on the whole quite calm. How wrong I was! I went to my cabin and gathered service books, Communion kit and suitable clothes, as I was to spend a few days on board *Grey Rover* and re-join *Plymouth* in Miami. Having got my kit together into a 'Pusser's grip' (canvas holdall) I made my way to the quarter deck from where the 'killick of the watch' would launch the RIB (Rigid Inflatable Boat). At that level the sea looked very rough indeed, so we climbed onto the craft and it was rather like sitting on a horse, with my feet in the stirrups and my bag clutched in front of me. The boat was hoisted up in the davits and lowered over the side. When the boat was lowered to within a couple of feet of the waves, the killick gave the thumbs up and the cleats were knocked out and we dropped with a bone shattering crunch. I had already been told to keep my tongue out of my teeth.

We immediately swung away from the ship's side and sped across the sea, bouncing from wave to wave. I could feel my lunch swilling around in my tummy! If I'd known that I was going to be doing this I would have had a salad! We came alongside *Grey Rover*, which was a grey wall towering above me, then a rope ladder was lowered together with a line and hook. I put my bag onto the hook and let it go. Whoever was on the other end of the line wasn't looking, as they were slow pulling my bag up when a wave cascaded over it before a shout from above and the bag shot up the ship's side. How I envied it!

Fortunately, my clothes were inside a black plastic bag and they were fine but the Communion set wasn't and my Prayer Book has salt stains to this day! The killick shouted above the noise of the engine and the sea, 'Bish, when I give you the word, slip your feet out of the stirrups and when I give you the thumbs up make a grab for the ladder', this was certainly not something I had in mind the day that I was Ordained! I took my feet out of the stirrups, gripping the handle in front of me with all my might, it was a truly a white knuckle ride. When his thumb went up I launched myself for the ladder and got two hands on and immediately the RIB roared away and I was left dangling on the side of *Grey Rover*. As I looked, to my horror, I saw a great big 'goffer' (large wave) rolling straight at me. I managed to scramble up a few rungs of the ladder and hung on when the wave struck.

It tried to pull me off the ladder but failed. After the initial shock was over I was able to continue my ascent up the ladder and onto the main deck, where I received a very good welcome. They were all a little concerned that I might have been swept away because I had no lifeline on but all was well. I found out later that on board *Plymouth* there was much hilarity at my plight and very little sympathy with predictable comments like, 'Next time try walking'.

I was given a warm welcome and shown to an enormous cabin with a double bed. The church service was quickly organized but sadly the only person who came was the Captain of the RFA. The entire ship's company totaled around 50 souls and they really weren't interested in Sunday worship, so my crossing had been just for one but as the Lord Jesus said, 'Where two or three are gathered in my Name I will be in the midst of them'.

That evening I dined alone because unlike the Royal Navy, RFA personnel are civilian and tend to have little social contact, at least, that's what happened in that ship. After supper the steward invited me to watch a film which I gratefully accepted, expecting to be joined by others. The film was 'Silver Bullet' with Gene Wilder, an hilarious film but I was on my own. In the RN Sunday night movies at sea are always well attended. Perhaps it was my after shave but it couldn't have been, as I had a beard!

Over the next couple of days I got around the ship and met nearly everyone. I was curious as to what they did in the evenings and I discovered that they did a myriad of different things from building model aircraft to radio hamming. Two days later we arrived in Miami and I walked along the jetty to re-join *Plymouth* from what had been an interesting interlude.

We sailed from Miami on the Friday for passage to Nassau, which we reached the following day and from there we sailed for the Dominican Republic, where our voyage took a turn for the worse.

The Dominican Republic is half of an island, the other half being Haiti, and we put into Port of Spain. The standard cocktail party was held but late on in the evening, after everyone had left, we were having a 'night cap' in the Wardroom when the Officer of Day came in and said there was a man on the gangway asking to see the senior officer. This happened to be a Peter Plum, the Captain being ashore. Peter asked that he be shown down to the wardroom but he first asked the Officer of the Day, 'Any idea what it's about?' He replied, 'I think there has been an incident ashore'. So, the man was shown down to the Wardroom and he said, 'One of your sailors has been shot'. It caused instant pandemonium. Having discovered that the sailor was in the local hospital we very quickly located the Leading Medical Assistant (LMA), known as 'Doc', and asked for directions to the hospital. The man very kindly offered to take us there so, upon instruction from the first Lieutenant this unknown man kindly took the Doc and I to the hospital in a battered old Volkswagen Beetle.

When we arrived at the hospital the scene was unusual to say the least. I know the NHS in this country comes in for its fair share of stick but here there were dogs running around in the reception area and chickens too, and it was hot, humid and sticky. They could see we were from the ship so they called a doctor whose English was much better than my Spanish. He said, 'I will take you to him' but we still did not know who it was. As we walked along the doctor was talking to a nurse and I caught the word 'morte' and I said to the Doc, 'He's dead'.

Turning a corner, we saw a trolley or gurney, as the Americans call it, and on it was the body of young John

Christie, stripped to the waist. There were a number of bullet holes in him which had been plugged with cotton wool and his torso was smeared in blood. There had been obviously been attempts to wipe him down. There were plain clothed policemen standing near the trolley, poking the body and I lost my temper. I shouted at them to leave him alone. They had guns sticking out of their pockets and I discovered later that they were secret police, but I didn't care. Nobody was going to treat one of my sailors like that.

They shrugged and walked off and I told the LMA to get back to the ship to collect the 'Buffer' (Chief Bosuns Mate) and whomever and whatever was necessary to get him back on board. 'I'll stay here', I said, 'I'm not going to leave him but be as quick as you can, I don't trust these people.' I was afraid that the Dominican authorities, embarrassed by this incident and anxious to make a goodwill visit acceptable, would spirit the body away. Funny things go through your mind when secret police are involved. I knelt and said prayers for him, watched all the time by these secret policemen. I then sat in a chair that I had found and waited with him until the Buffer came with a couple of hands. We managed to lift him onto a sheet of heavy duty rubber as, it seemed, we had no ready-made body bags. The Buffer then produced a needle and palm and he was sewn into a make shift body bag and carried him out to the mini bus allocated to the ship, and then back to the ship.

John Christie had only joined the ship just before we

began the deployment, there being a need for a hand of his specialisation, and he had volunteered, so he wasn't really all that well known. Nevertheless, to have one of our own shot dead in such circumstances stunned everyone. Apparently, as he didn't have many mates on board, he had gone ashore on his own as soon as leave was piped. Outside the dockyard gates he came across an 'authorized' guide. These were people who had a licence to act as official guides and who required payment. Whether John failed to grasp this or not we will never know. He went with this guide, paid for his petrol, paid for his drinks and meals but late on in the evening around 2300, when they got back to the dockyard, he had asked for his money. As John did not realise that he had to pay him, he refused, so the man just pulled a pistol and shot him several times. As I sat by his body I thought, 'What a terrible, terrible, tragic waste of a young life'. Obviously, it blighted the rest of our visit to the Dominican Republic and the consulate were very anxious to try to make sure that the right things were done. We held a memorial service on the fo'cstle of *Plymouth* before we sailed, which was the very least we could do.

It was decided that I would go home, as the family had requested a Naval presence at John's funeral, which would be me and personnel from *Ariadne*. John Christie's body was taken by *Grey Rover* to Miami where the local coroner had insisted on having it thawed out so that a post mortem could take place to establish the cause of death, before allowing the body to travel to Washington.

From there it was flown home, arriving on Christmas Eve. The coroner of the West Midlands insisted on another post mortem and, as a result, no funeral could take place until the New Year.

Plymouth sailed on to St. Petersburg, as scheduled but I travelled home to the UK to attend the funeral where I was joined by the First Lieutenant of *Ariadne*. The Christie family was, of course, desperate to know what had happened but I couldn't go into any great detail, it would have been too difficult for them but they showed great kindness to us and were very grateful for our presence. The local vicar was also very kind and we shared the funeral service. After a reception we took our leave and returned to Portsmouth. For us, the end of a very sad event but not the end for his family.

I was due to leave the Squadron at the end of January but there was one other task that I had to do before I could go and that was to take the Bishop of Portsmouth to sea. I had talked to the Bishop, Timothy Bavin, on a number of occasions about having first-hand experience of life in a warship and he was very keen to do so but this was the first opportunity we had had to make it happen.

I invited him for a day at sea with the 6th Frigate Squadron on board *Achilles*. It was just a day out but he was able to tour the ship, speak to sailors, have lunch in the Junior Ratings Dining Hall and tea in the Wardroom and in between time observe a light jack-stay transfer, the method used to pass people from one ship to another. What happens is that the passenger sits in a chair which is pulled by ropes across the water from one ship to another. The Bishop was very keen to have a go but I was not too happy, as I had seen things go wrong and people getting dunked in the 'oggin'. I didn't think it was a good idea for the Bishop of Portsmouth to be dumped in the ocean. He would have probably taken it in his stride but there could well have been serious repercussions, so I persuaded him not to volunteer. Despite this, he enjoyed his time at sea, he saw the Navy in action, as much as possible in a day but it cemented in him the knowledge that the Navy was very much part of his diocese, and we enjoyed his company and his ministry. As he left the ship, on the jetty he turned and gave his Blessing on the ship, which I thought was rather nice and an excellent way for me to sign off with the squadron.

The following day, 29 January, I left the 6th Frigate Squadron and, following a period of leave, I took up my appointment as Chaplain to *HMS Nelson*, the main barracks in Portsmouth. My sea time had come to an end, for now and for the next few years it was to be a shore-based ministry.

Chapter Eighteen

HMS Nelson

HMS Nelson, is the main barracks for the Portsmouth Command area. It used to be called HM Naval Base as the full base included the dockyard. The dockyard is the area that maintains and services the ships. The barracks maintains and services the sailors and a wall divides them. Ships undergoing re-fit or a maintenance period would be in dry dock or alongside and the sailors working in them would need somewhere to live whilst the work progressed, since all living facilities on board would be shut down. So, it was the practice that they would go into work in the morning and then in the evening return to barracks to 'dhobi' (shower) and eat.

In addition, it was a transit camp, accommodating people who were waiting for a 'draft' or going outside or one of the myriad of reasons for the to-ing and fro-ing of life in the Navy.

Nelson was created and built during the height of Empire and some of its buildings still bear that imperial stamp. The site is divided by Queen Street, on one side is the Wardroom, which is a very imperial building, and on the other side is the main body of the establishment and includes accommodation blocks for senior and junior ratings, blocks for the main administration offices including those of the commanding officer (a commodore) and Heads of Departments, the pay office, sick bay, dental surgery, clothing and general stores, main galley and education. There was also a motor pool, a NAAFI and barber shop. The offices of the Naval Personal and Family Service (NPFS) were also here but with access from the outside, so families could have meetings with social workers without having to go through the main gate and security.

In my time I had a great deal to do with NPFS and became very friendly with the people there who did a great job. The older blocks, which were originally built for accommodation, were now used for other things. Hardy Block housed the gymnasium and the PTI office with lecture rooms and library on the second floor. Whilst Rodney Block had some lecture rooms and storage facilities, the ground floor housed the chaplaincy.

There were three chaplains during my time – me, as the Church of England chaplain, Frank Beattie, the Church of Scotland Free Church chaplain, who was actually United Reformed, and the Roman Catholic chaplain, who I believe was Michael Morrissey. The Verger's name was Madge, I can't remember her surname but she was marvellous, nothing was ever too much trouble for her and she would always put herself out for others at any time. At a later date she was awarded the MBE for her services to the Royal Navy.

I was to relieve Rev'd Trevor Lynn, a very experienced

chaplain who had been around the Navy for some time, so it was important that I listened to him as, though the work of the Naval chaplain doesn't differ from ship to shore, the detail does.

When I arrived I had an interview with the Commodore and was then taken around the different departments and introduced to the Heads of Department. This done, we adjourned to the office to talk about the tasks that I would face. Being chaplain to *Nelson* was a very busy job from Monday to Friday but there were very few services on a Sunday. Largely because on Friday afternoon it was like the starting grid of the Le Mans, when most would go on weekend leave. Usually, the only people who were on board was the Duty Watch.

Once a month there was a service of Holy Communion in the chapel, attended by members of the Portsmouth Retired Naval Officers Association and their wives. They would then have lunch in the Wardroom. There was the occasional baptism in chapel and on board those ships which were in refit or undergoing a maintenance period or whose chaplains were away.

Nelson's chaplains not only looked after the barracks but also the satellite units, of which there were a number. These were outlying stations which were too small to have chaplains appointed to them so they came under our 'umbrella'. These 'lodger' units included *HMS Phoenix*, the damage control school, where I had attended a first aid course not long before; the Fire Fighting school at Port Solent; the former torpedo school at *HMS Vernon* (now Gun Wharf Quays); Whale Island (the former Gunnery School);and *HMS Temeraire*, the PT school. All of these were cared for, pastorally, by *Nelson*'s chaplains. In practice that meant we conducted prayers at each of these units usually once a month.

My colleagues were also responsible for other establishments which had their own CofE chaplains, so we were all very busy. There was not a great deal of ecumenical worship but we had occasional chaplains' meetings to discuss what was happening within *Nelson* and to allocate the weekly prayer 'slots' at the outer units and in *Nelson,* because there was a weekly service in the chapel.

These services were sponsored by different departments. They were short and usually at the start of the day, a sort of 'Thought for the Day' with prayers. At very least it kept us in touch with people. Attendance at these prayers varied considerably not least due to some of these establishments being run down. For example, Whale Island had a ship's company of just 20 people, so we might only get a dozen at prayers. 'Whaley' was also home to the Regulating School and they too had prayers on a monthly basis but these were well-attended. A The headquarters of the Sea Cadet Corps was also located on 'Whaley' and whenever a course was present at a weekend we were asked to provide a short service for them.

Another duty was to cover the chaplains in St Ann's when they took leave, which meant taking services on

Sunday, committals of ashes, weddings and baptisms.

Without doubt, the unit that took up a great deal of time was the Detention Quarters (DQ), the Navy's prison. Built in Edwardian times it was designed as a prison of its day but each man had his own room (we were not allowed to call them cells) and the paintwork was fresh and bright. There was a fully-equipped gymnasium and the food was excellent but there was a standard of discipline. Misdemeanors in the Royal Navy were punished at Captain's Table or in very serious cases by court martial. Very, very serious cases went to Colchester to serve out their sentence prior to dismissal but most ended up in DQs. The aim was to get them 'back on the rails' and back to work. The 'Cat o' Nine Tails' used for flogging had long since disappeared as a means of discipline

Every Monday in DQs there was a staff meeting to discuss the week ahead, who was arriving and who was departing. Then on Wednesday morning there would be prayers at Divisions. On Friday, new arrivals would be interviewed, this was not compulsory as far as chaplains were concerned but encouraged. Then on Sundays at 0900 there would be a service in the little chapel, which again was not compulsory but encouraged.

From time to time we could be called in on other matters. I'll give you one example. I received a phone call late one forenoon from DQs asking me to attend. On arrival I found the staff gathered in the main office and it was quickly explained that one of the inmates had lost his temper violently and had, in their words, 'smashed up his room and refused to let them in' and he was not coming out; furthermore he was going on hunger strike so, 'F… the lot of you and f…the Royal Navy'. To try to overpower him was not an option because there was little space in the room and it meant somebody would get hurt. To be fair, the staff were all in their late 50s and not that fit. They looked at me and said, 'Would you have a word?' So we went into the block, all other inmates having been confined to their rooms, and as I started up the stairs two members said, 'We'll come with you'. 'No' I replied, one sight of you and he'll kick off again'. 'But you might get hurt'. 'No', I replied, 'if he hurts me he'll get seven years bad luck. It'll be OK'

The door to his room was standing ajar, so I knocked and called out, 'Jimmy, it's the Bish, I'm coming in if that's OK?' I pushed open the door and the room was in a mess. He'd overturned his bed, tossed aside his table over and thrown items around. His knuckles were bleeding from hitting the wall. 'Blimey Jim, what's brought this on?' says I. 'It's those bastards', he said, 'they added a week on to my sentence'. 'Why?' I asked but already knew. 'Because my kit wasn't up to scratch. My bloody kit, that's all'. 'Mind if I sit down?' I asked and we both looked around and both started to laugh. 'Come on', I said, 'you can't live like this. What would your mother say?',

We straightened out the room as best we could, I sat down, pulled out a packet of cigarettes and offered him one. 'We are not allowed to smoke in here,' he said, 'Yeah, I know but just what are they going to do to me?' 'Don't you like the Navy?' I asked and he said, 'Love it but I hate it here. I can't see my girlfriend and I can't box'. 'Why can't you box in here, the gym's got the kit?' So we talked and I pointed out that the quickest way to see his girlfriend and get back to proper boxing was to do his time. 'They don't want to keep you any longer than they have to so, do yourself a favour, just do what you're told to do. You are like a truck that's come off the rails and all they are trying to do here is get you back on the rails, so why not give them a hand?' You'll get extra time for all of this but if you apologize and offer to pay for any damages it won't be that bad. You're a big boy, you can do this standing on your head. I'll give your girlfriend a ring, if you like, and explain'. He said, 'Thanks Bish, I'd appreciate it'. I went back down, explained about the cigarette smoke and said, 'He'll be fine now'. And he was.

That gives a general idea of my duties. I can see no point in giving a day by day account of my time in *Nelson*. I can only speak for the CofE but most clergy worth their salt had extremely busy schedules and their diaries would be as 'rammed' as mine were, it's just that my parish was slightly different from the 'norm'.

In addition to the pastoral duties we had a social life in HMS *Nelson* and its satellites, such as Wardroom socials, Summer balls and Christmas dances. Bonfire Night was held at Whaley and Naval families enjoyed the occasions, when it didn't rain.

During my time at *Nelson* I once again had the privilege of serving under John Tolhurst (he was CO of the *Berwick* mentioned in a previous chapter and my first book) now a Commodore. It was the second time we'd served together. He is a gentleman, courteous and kind but with an extremely sharp mind and more than a hint of steel when he needed it, and a very ready smile.

Because of its transitory nature I rarely had the opportunity to get alongside the sailors and get to know them as I would have in a ship but I was able to get around the establishment and meet people. Having done several courses in the Education Block, it was nice to see old chums and catch up with what they had been doing. Calling in to the gym and 'making my number' with the PTIs was also a pleasure.

Nelson hosted a number of inter Service competitions like one memorable Navy v RAF boxing tournament. These were 'pukka' occasions and officers wore Mess dress but I used to enjoy sitting amongst the sailors in clerical rig, as these were occasions when I could.

I remember one heavyweight bout, the last of the evening. 'Ladies and Gentlemen,' called the referee, 'the last bout of the evening between, in the Blue corner, representing the Royal Air Force, Leading Aircraftsman Davis.' LAC Davis was immaculate in what looked like silk vest and shorts with a blue sash and proper boxing boots and he came smartly to attention. 'And in the Red corner, representing the Royal Navy, Leading Cook Richards.' L/C Richards also came smartly to attention but there the similarity ended, for he was dressed in a white vest and black shorts and wore a pair of 'daps'(gym shoes). There was a great deal of ribald comment from the sailors but I had found out that L/C Richards had only arrived back in Portsmouth that afternoon as he was serving in HMS *Intrepid*. All his kit had been lost and nothing in the PTI store fitted him. Not only that but he had a bit of a paunch! Keeping fit at sea is not easy and Naval chefs work very hard, up early and bed late. I feared that this would be a walk over.

The bell sounded and LAC Davis was up on his toes and looked every inch the winner, whilst L/C Richards wasn't doing much 'dancing'. He survived the first round with much encouragement from the crowd but he nevertheless, took a pounding. He may not look much but he was Navy after all! He was having a bit of a boxing lesson and looked to be very tired as he tried to catch the airman, who was dancing rings around him. Then as we approached the end of the second round Richards threw a haymaker of a left hook, which landed squarely on the airman's jaw and he hit the canvas with a crash. He was counted out and the place erupted. I went around to the dressing rooms after the fight and spoke to the winners and 'runners up' (I don't like the term 'loser' in boxing because it takes a great deal of courage to get into the ring in the first place!) and I spoke to L/C Richards and said 'That was a great punch'. He replied, 'Bish, I was knackered, out on my feet, it was then or never'. It just goes to show that looks aren't everything!

Another incident that lives in my memory but not so humorous took place on Friday, 22 September 1989. I arrived in my office at the normal 0800 and said Morning Prayer. I was going through Daily Orders when the phone rang and it was Michael Bucks who asked if I'd heard the news. Apparently a bomb had gone off in the Royal Marine School of Music at Deal in Kent. The chaplain of the school was Charles Howard, who was on a sailing course somewhere in the English Channel and couldn't be contacted, so I was told to round up my colleagues and get across to RM barracks at Eastney where we were to be taken to Deal to help. There followed a quick flurry of phone calls and a car appeared to take us over to Eastney. We couldn't locate the RC chaplain anywhere, so Frank Beattie and I grabbed our coats and went. We were joined by two members of the NPFS.

Taking off from the helipad, we arrived in Deal a short time later. We found that the assistant chaplains (who were local clergy) had been doing a great job in counselling and comforting the young bandsmen, nearly all teenagers, and had gathered them into their barrack rooms. At least those that weren't damaged.

Because they were civvies they were unsure as to the next steps to take, so I went to see the Bandmaster and suggested that these young people be sent home immediately, which would get them off the site and they could be comforted at home. 'Could you see to that,' he said, 'as I'm snowed under?' So I went back to the barrack rooms and told them all to phone their parents to see who could be collected. Those who could not be collected were issued warrants, which I collected from the RSM's office. They were all gone fairly swiftly.

That morning most of the school had already been in classrooms or on the parade ground, practicing marching and playing. They all saw the effects of this enormous explosion, which was heard many miles away and rattled windows the other side of Deal. They saw the buildings collapse and a number of them were traumatized for some time afterwards.

The damage was extensive to both people and property, 11 Royal Marines were killed and 21 seriously injured, many of them trapped in the rubble of the buildings for hours until lifting equipment and rescue workers could get to them. One of those trapped was the bandsman who had served with me on board *HMS Fife*. He was blown into a locker and had to wait until rescuers got to him but I was able to talk to him later that day. I saw him months later when he came to serve with the Portsmouth band and asked how he was and he said that he was still getting 'coffin dreams'. He was a very lucky chap because all around him were killed, the locker had saved him.

Throughout the day we spent time talking to families who had come to collect their sons and to those bandsmen who had survived, giving what counselling we could to rescuers and rescued alike. The Commandant General Royal Marines, Sir Martin Garrod and Lady

Garrod came in the late forenoon. Their presence gave encouragement to all and they spoke to as many people as they could including me. He had been my commanding officer in 40 Commando and was a delightful man. They did a lot of good that day.

Eventually things began to stabilize to the point where we could do no more, Charlie Howard had been contacted and was on his way back.

As the helicopter that had brought us to Deal was no longer available, we hired a car and drove back to *Nelson*. It was an extreme pastoral experience and one that will always live long with me. I learned a great deal from it. Another indication of the duties that we had to perform at the drop of a hat.

In July 1989 the annual Amport Conference was held. This was something I always enjoyed. The Chaplain of the Fleet had changed and the post was now held by my old boss at St Ann's, Michael Henley, who interviewed all the chaplains individually. When my turn came he said, 'You are due a move, so I'd like you to take over *Collingwood*'. I was stunned and said 'But that's a very senior appointment, I haven't got enough time in'. 'You have as far as I'm concerned' and that was that. My time as chaplain to *HMS Nelson* ended on Friday 22 December and I was to take up my new appointment in the New Year.

Chapter Nineteen

HMS Collingwood

HMS *Collingwood*, a 'stone frigate,' was created and commissioned on 10 January 1940, initially to instruct 'hostilities only' ratings of the Seaman's Branch.

It was a vast area covered in wooden huts, used for accommodation and instruction, with a large parade ground.

Wireless telegraphy ratings started their training there in June 1940 and a Radio Direction Finding school (radar) was added in 1942. After the war it was decided that *Collingwood* would become the main training establishment for electrical ratings in the Fleet.

As weaponry changed from shells to missiles, this training also took place at *Collingwood* and it became known as the Weapons Electrical School. Today it is known as the Maritime Warfare Centre which incorporates many other disciplines.

The wooden huts are long gone, except the church, and it became a very modern, functional establishment. Because of its practical nature and appearance, it looked like a small town in Eastern Europe and became known, affectionately, as 'Collingrad'.

I took up my appointment on 11 January 1990. There

was a handover with the outgoing chaplain, which was completed on the 16th when I became chaplain to HMS *Collingwood*.

The chaplaincy had, more or less, the same arrangement that we had in my previous job. I was the Church of England chaplain and I had CSFC and RC colleagues and a verger, a lady named Doreen Stewart. She was, of course, a civil servant and had been at the chaplaincy for some time and was, as a result, a 'fount of all knowledge'.

There were a number of differences between *Nelson* and *Collingwood* in terms of chaplaincy work, principally, there were no lodger units. In *Nelson* there were outlying units and I spent a great deal of time travelling to these units, visiting and taking prayers. In *Collingwood* it was very much 'in house' by that I mean, the day-to-day routine was conducted within the parameters of the establishment itself. Of course, there were things like hospital visiting and baptismal visits but by and large from Monday to Friday, the majority of work was within the establishment itself.

In *Collingwood* I had regular church services. Every Sunday at 1030 we had a celebration of Holy Communion with hymns, attended by a regular congregation, which included families, and in turn this meant we were able to hold Sunday School for the children. This was run by their mothers on a rotational basis and the chaplaincy provided the equipment and resources they needed.

In the summer we went on a picnic to Hambledon Country Park and invited other members of their families to join us. There were also baptisms of children of those who served in *Collingwood*, many of whom lived locally. They were encouraged to contact the local clergy to keep them informed that a baptism from within their parish was to take place and that they approved.

Another major difference was that in *Collingwood*, it being a training establishment so there was a great deal of teaching to be done. We had classes virtually every day, instructing the apprentices and trainees on such subjects as morality and religion. Most of them had never been to church but because they were apprentices in the Navy they were part of the training policy that the Navy had at that time titled 'The Whole Man'. This meant that those who joined would be developed physically, mentally and spiritually. There was a lot of sport and physical recreation but we tried to inculcate into them the concept of God and His dealings with mankind and their role in it.

It is difficult in this day and age to encourage young men to take seriously that concept of religion and morality but nevertheless we had to try. Our talks covered such topics as the Geneva Convention, pacifism and how the Christian faith worked in the modern world, with particular emphasis on the Royal Navy. These talks would be illustrated with videos and films and would lead on to discussion.

Sometimes we would have one class to talk to or there

could be four or five, it all depended on the training programme. My CSFC colleague and I shared the talks we had to give but the Roman Catholics would fall out and be seen by the RC chaplain in his smaller lecture room to one side of his office. We also had divisions three days a week on Tuesdays, Wednesdays and Thursdays which were again shared between us. Once a term, on a Friday afternoon, there would be Ceremonial Divisions which meant that the troops would be in best uniform and I would turn to in choir robes (cassock, surplice, scarf and hood). There was usually a VIP to inspect the Guard of Honour, and on completion of Divisions, the establishment went on leave.

We also had visits from different people, like theological students who came to look at the role of the chaplain in the Naval environment, and medical students who came to look at the establishment and I talked to them on the role of the chaplain in terms of links with the sick bay and the overall process of healing.

We also had visits from potential chaplains. 30 years ago, as I write, a certain Andrew Hillier came to see me in *Collingwood* and he's now Chaplain of the Fleet, another was one John Greene. He and his wife visited through an 'aquaint' visit and he too became Chaplain of the Fleet, so I was privileged to be part of the stepping stones that these two men had in their ministries.

To further advance the concept of the 'Whole Man' there were very extensive sports facilities within the establishment, including a first-class swimming pool and

Sports Club, pitches to cater for all team sports but also an excellent outward bound facility.

I was given to understand that many years before, a former Captain of *Collingwood* lived in the Brecon Beacons at the time when Dr Beeching (Transport Minister) was wielding his 'axe' on the railway system of Great Britain. The line between Talybont and Brecon had been closed but the old Station Master's house at Talybont was up for sale. The Captain thought that it would make a very good outward bound centre, so he bought it and gave it to *HMS Collingwood*. I don't know if it is still in use but in my time it was a tremendous asset and it was well used by those under training. The training staff would stay in the house, the troops would be under canvas around the house and people like me, who would visit for a day or so would stay locally.

The time spent in the Brecon Beacons was hugely important for the young people, particularly those from inner-city areas, as it was a complete change from their normal environment. I remember being with a group on a map-reading exercise when we came across a cairn which had been erected by local people in memory of the crew of a 'Wellington' bomber that had crashed there in 1943 with the loss of six young Canadian airmen. It was a salutary lesson for these young sailors because they realized that many years before, other young men gave their lives in the defence of freedom.

Collingwood was a huge establishment with many different departments and therefore to try to get around them all was quite a job but I tried. Pastorally it was important to take an interest in what people did and it was certainly one way of engaging with them. Visiting during 'Stand Easy' and having a cup of tea with different groups was also a way of projecting the chaplaincy into the general working life of the establishment.

The 'lectures' that we delivered on the moral and spiritual side of life were part of the overall training schedule within the establishment. Occasionally we would get a phone call saying that a particular class couldn't turn up and the training staff would rearrange the period.

I was never happy about the type of material that we had available, I thought it outdated. When talking to young people, you have to be able to engage with them and to hold their attention. So I began to look at what was available in the wider Church. At the Christian Resources Exhibition, I was delighted to find an awful lot of information about communication with young people. On my return I contacted the chaplains in *HMS Sultan* to find out what they did and I also got in touch with Bagshot Park, at that time the home of the Royal Army Chaplains Department. Through them I was passed on to the Junior Leaders Training Office. They were very kind and they invited me to attend Bagshot Park which I duly did. I was there overnight and they showed me the material they used in teaching their young soldiers.

I was very impressed. I returned to *Collingwood* and discussed matters with my colleagues and we agreed that we ought to update the entire visual aids that we had. I then went to see the Director of Training (DoT) and told him and I discovered in the course of the discussion that we were at least twelve periods down on what was originally allocated to the chaplaincy. These periods had been allowed to erode over time and when I asked why, I was told these periods were needed for sport. I said, 'I know sport is important but what we are trying to do is important too. I'd like them back please, especially as we are trying to improve what we do with these young men'. He replied, 'Can't be done, I'm afraid'. So, I went to the Captain and protested, the Captain said, 'Give me the revamped programme that you're hoping for and then we'll see what we can do'.

I thought that there should be a more realistic approach to what we were trying to do in view of the fact that we were part of the overall training package. At Bagshot Park it was pointed out that Britain had changed and the Armed Forces, like other organizations, draws their recruits from within this changing society. Therefore if we were to give them a good background then they needed to know what other people believed.

The young men that we talked to would eventually become Leading Hands in charge of mess decks or they could become president of a mess, and as such, they should be aware of the variety of people under their care and the beliefs those people held.

As part of the changes envisaged, I proposed an outline of the other religions held within Britain, a 'thumbnail sketch' of Islam, Judaism, Buddhism but the vast majority of our time would be on Christianity and the moral values based on this. I took this revamped programme to the Captain and the DoT attended as well. The Captain said, 'I agree, make it so'.

The DoT grumbled about giving back twelve periods but in the end we settled on six in the spirit of compromise. I outlined these ideas to my colleagues who seemed to accept them but little did I know that they told their Principal Chaplains that I intended teaching these other religions. They objected to it but without telling me.

The Principals went to the Chaplain of the Fleet and the first I knew about it was when on 7 September, the Staff Chaplain came to lunch and asked me, 'How do you fancy going to sea in *Invincible* as your next job?' I said, 'I'd love to'. He said, 'Fine, well we should look for a date in November'. I assumed he was talking about November the following year, so I said 'November next year'? 'No, this year'. I said, 'You're talking about two months time?' 'Yes, Rob Nurton has come to the end of his time in the ship and needs to move and there's no one available to relieve him'. I said, 'But I'm not available, I've only been here nine months and, subject to approval, we are hoping to change the teaching arrangements' 'Well, somebody else will have to do that as the 'Boss' thinks you are the best candidate'.

And that was that!

I had less than a year in *Collingwood*. I was bemused and very disappointed because, in effect, I was sacked. I had obviously failed to convince my colleagues or they had completely misunderstood my motives but there it was. It was very sad and I thought it a lost opportunity because I don't think anything was done to get those lectures back and I left *Collingwood* on 8 November after just ten months. I was sorry to go because I liked *Collingwood* and still do but 'every cloud'... I was off to sea again, probably for the last time.

Chapter Twenty

HMS Invincible

HMS Invincible was the Royal Navy's lead ship of her class, the first of three light aircraft carriers. She was launched on 3 May 1977 and was the seventh ship to carry the name. Originally designated as a 'through deck cruiser', because the Navy didn't build aircraft carriers any more, nevertheless she carried Sea Harrier strike aircraft and Sea King helicopters which had either an anti-submarine role or acted as early warning radar.

After the Falklands War she was fitted with 30 mm 'Goalkeeper' close support weapon systems which were extremely good: they could track multiple targets at the range of 5 miles. They were very accurate. The pilots, when flying, were keen to ensure that the systems remained off!

When *HMS Hermes* was sold to India, *Invincible* became the capital ship of the Royal Navy. The ship's company numbered 600 but when the air group was embarked the number went up to 1200. It was my great privilege to be appointed her chaplain.

I joined *Invincible* on Tuesday, 13 November 1990 and, as always, there had to be a handover which was to last a few days. The chaplain that I was relieving, the Rev'd

Robert Nurton, had organized an extensive and very efficient handover. The handover commenced in his cabin known, unsurprisingly, as 'The Vicarage' and he talked to me about the ship and its people before taking me to meet the Captain, who was no stranger to me, nor I to him.

This would be the third time that I had served under the command of Captain John Tolhurst. He welcomed me with a broad smile and we talked, briefly, about how he saw my role within the ship and that I would always have his support. It was a great start.

There followed introductions and brief conversations with the Commander, John Rimington and the other Heads of Departments (HODs) and their deputies. Though I had not served with any of them before, I had served with John Rimington's brother-in-law who had been First Lieutenant of *Ariadne* (See *'Onward Christian Sailors'*).

Then came a tour of the ship and its various departments, the names came thick and fast and disappeared from my mind equally as quickly. No doubt I would get used to it all in due course. Then we began to sign over all the accounts and items that were held by the chaplain relating to the chapel and all the other areas of responsibility.

There had been a number of applications for baptism which Rob had held over since he was leaving, so an early task for me was to contact the fathers of the children concerned and introduce myself. It was a great way of getting around the ship and becoming known by the people.

Once the hand over was complete, Rob took his leave and I had the daunting task of finding my way around by myself. Compared to the frigates that I had served in she was a big ship. Today, of course, the Navy's aircraft carriers are three times as big and I would love to be the chaplain to *Queen Elizabeth* or *Prince of Wales* but I'm 'past my sell by date!'

There were a number of meetings that I had to attend including a HODs meeting in the commander's cabin to look at future events that applied to the ship and included 'Link Families'. This was a system whereby should it become necessary, information would be passed to the Captain's wife and she would contact the wives of Department Heads who would then pass it on. So the information would cascade to all members of the ship's company as a result of one phone call. I gathered that I would be responsible for keeping the contact numbers up to date.

Meetings are a two way street, so I was able to inform them of my hopes for services including the upcoming Christmas service, my use of Daily Orders, and use of the vestry and the chapel.

Now, the chapel was only part of a compartment known as the 'Chapel/Schoolroom'. It was the lowest compartment in the ship, right above the propeller shafts. On one side, screened off by curtains, was a storage/baggage compartment. The Altar was contained in a small recess which was also curtained off when not in use and the remainder was covered in desks and chairs which could be quickly rearranged for services.

I mentioned using Daily Orders because I used to announce Saints days and chapel services as well as other 'dits'. It was a good way of keeping in the 'public eye'.

On Wednesday 12 December we sailed to test systems. The ship had been alongside for a while so it was necessary to get to sea and put systems to the test, especially new members of the ships company, including the WRENS. *Invincible* was not the first ship to have women as part of the ships company but it was my first experience of women at sea.

In early January we sailed to continue the 'shake down' in the Channel, the main aim being to test the ships company. This short time at sea enabled people to get used to the changes.

The day to day routines of the Navy are common to most ships, the only difference is the size and frequency. For example, on board *Invincible* the day began at 0700 with 'Call the Hands' (a 'pipe' made over the main broadcast, a sort of Naval alarm clock) and then the Systems Operating Check (the alarms go off from different locations) and then the working day commences. Perhaps there would be staff meetings or other administrative factors as well as the usual maintenance of the ship and the aircraft. My day would begin like everyone else's, I would say Morning Prayer, then deal with any administration that might need my attention and then go on a walk around the parish. Stopping at the NAAFI to talk to the 'can man' and then go on to the Regulating Office (the police station) and talk to the 'crushers', have a cup of coffee with them and then on to the engineering control room and on up to the bridge. As I walked, invariably I would be stopped and fall into conversation with any number of people, just like a normal parish. Throw into the mix teaching NAMET and/or GCSE English, marking essays or journals, organising the schedule for TV and radio, mid-day Eucharists and you have a busy sort of day.

Speaking of mid-day Eucharists, the chapel was right above the propellers and if, during the service, the Officer of the Watch decided to increase revolutions the noise and vibration levels increased dramatically. I frequently had to make a grab for the chalice as it bounced across the altar. Usually, a quick phone call from the vestry was followed by an apology and we continued with the celebration. I sometimes wondered if it was done to 'wind up the vicar!' Surely not? Writing letters was usually done when there was a gap in duties or late on in the day.

A few days after joining the ship, on entering the Wardroom ante-room, I was approached by three senior officers, the Air Engineer, Christopher 'Kit' Davidson, the Senior Medical Officer, Phil Runchman and the Dental Officer, Neil Harkness. They sidled up to me very furtively and asked if I drank alcohol and after some thought I said that I did, occasionally. They then said that they would be honoured if I would join a little club that they had. I was filled with apprehension, it was called 'The Sundowners' and it met most evenings in one of the cabins. Whoever's cabin it was, provided the pre-dinner drinks and 'nibbles'. It was an opportunity to discuss the day's events or anything else. Becoming chums with senior people would give me access to their departments much more easily, besides it was a kind gesture of welcome and I readily accepted their invitation. From time to time other guests would be invited, which made it all the more interesting.

Something else that happened in my early days on board was an invitation from the Captain to be one of the Entertainment Officers, the other being the Dental Officer, Neil Harkness. He asked me to have particular oversight of looking after the television and radio and organizing the programmes that went out each evening. So often the evenings would find me in the studio with the other volunteers who would run the studio. Programme planning and schedules depended on the ship's programme and it was a communal activity but with me having the final word. The 'rule of thumb' was, no porn, no smut and nothing to upset the Wrens! We tried to run both TV and radio on fairly conventional lines and I let it be known via Daily Orders that if anyone would like to run a programme or had any ideas, to let me know and we would do our best to accommodate them.

For example two Royal Marines had their own radio

programme with some banter in between music, when they got it wrong, they were told.

People could request music of all sorts which was duly played provided we had it on board. It wasn't all pop music, we had classical programmes too. I had audio tapes sent from home which included recordings of 'The Archers' They were always about two or three weeks behind but nevertheless they were always looked forward to. It was bit like Radio 4, the news at 1900 which came in from the MOD each evening, followed by 'The Archers' and the rest of the programmes followed on.

What surprised me was the number of the younger people who were keen on 'The Archers'. On one occasion, a newly joined Midshipman asked me how we were able to get 'The Archers' when we were in the South China Sea, 'Easy' I said, 'just tune in to Radio 4'; 'I tried that but I can't get it'. 'Never mind', says I, 'just listen to *Invincible'* radio instead'. I also had with me the BBC's version of 'The Lord of the Rings' and played that as a serial.

I held a celebration of Holy Communion at 1230 in the chapel each day depending on the ships programmes and then on Sunday morning there would be a 0830 celebration of Holy Communion in the chapel and a 1030 service in the Junior Ratings Dining Hall (JRDH) or on the Quarter Deck depending on the sea state or the weather conditions. It would be unlikely to be held on the Quarterdeck in the North Atlantic but highly likely in the Caribbean.

We had a ship's band who were quite good but who were coming along even better under the baton of a colour sergeant Royal Marines. From time to time we might even have the Royal Marines band on board but it was always the ship's company band that played at the church services. The 1030 service followed the pattern of a 'hymn/prayer sandwich' just as I done in other ships. These services would be sponsored by different departments, so I would have to get the readings to the department early in the week and then 'chivvy' them up for their choice of hymns so that the band could practice.

I would give them a steer as to the hymns for a particular Sunday but very often it was the favourite hymn of their grandmothers. It was not unusual to have 'Once in Royal David's City' sung in July! It was a neverending cycle, as soon as the services on the Sunday were over, on Monday morning you had to start preparing for the following week, again depending on where the ship was going to be at that time.

There were quite a lot of daily meetings which didn't involve me but there were the usual HODs meetings that happened from time to time and the Command Brief that happened each evening at 1800, usually on the Bridge. The Captain would receive daily reports from each of the departments delivered by the HOD or DHOD. I rarely had anything to say but it was always useful to be there to find out what was going on in the different departments and in the ship as a whole. *Invincible* also had, from time to time, midshipmen on board, cadets from

Dartmouth and their journals would require setting and marking. In other words, I was one of those who had to set the titles of essays and then mark the finished article.

That, hopefully, gives you an idea of the daily/weekly routines of life on board a large warship but as I mentioned earlier, we were in 'shakedown' mode, with a very high percentage of the ship's company who were new, especially the Wrens. So we had Nuclear, Biological, Chemical Defence (NBCD) exercises on board to test the capability of ship to shut down quickly in the event of an attack or in the event of an emergency.

The Command had to see how people reacted to a variety of circumstances which was very important, bearing in mind that the current news was of the Iraqi invasion of Kuwait, which was the prelude to the first Gulf War but more on the exercises later.

I was also a member of the newly re-formed welfare committee and regular meetings were to be held to discuss aspects of the ship's company social life, to include planning for events like a ship's company dance, providing sporting equipment and other facilities to enhance life on board. Speaking of aspects of sport, sailing in the English Channel meant that we were able to receive some TV programmes from land, including sporting fixtures.

Being a Welshman it was assumed that I liked rugby, I don't. Football is my game (and cricket) but when the Rugby Internationals were broadcast I came in for a huge amount of 'stick' because Wales were going through a dreadful patch. It was all good natured banter and I was big enough and ugly enough to take it.

Mess deck visiting was a part of my routine. I firmly believe in parish visiting. As a curate in Swansea, my vicar insisted that I carry out at least 15 visits a week. 'If they are not in, leave a card but our people must know that we are out and about caring for them. 'Remember this', he would say, 'A house-going parson makes for a church-going people.' He was right and it is something I have always ascribed to. Being in a warship made no difference, the principle was the same. Sadly, not much in evidence in the modern church and the results are to be seen! However, I would first approach the Mess president or the Leading hand and seek an invitation, I wouldn't just drop in as it was their home, and I would try to never outstay my welcome. Sometimes if a discussion was going on I would see it through but usually my visits were never more than a pair of hours.

We were back alongside in Portsmouth on 25 January for a Harbour Week during which time GCSE teaching continued and the NAMET exams took place. The opportunity was taken for sport and the ship's rugby team played that of *HMS Birmingham* at the Burnaby Road sports ground and again two days later we played *Birmingham* at football.

I can't remember the outcomes but I went along to support both teams. The ship's company had a lecture on Sea Survival held in the hangar and the same evening there was a Ladies Night in the wardroom when the wives or girlfriends of the officers come on board and dined as our guests. They were very pleasant occasions and it gave us an opportunity to entertain our wives and partners in a formal setting, thanking them for all that they did and the support they gave. Harbour Weeks also mean that I tended not to hold services on board but it was an opportunity to clean the chapel and vestry, which I did personally, and checked on supplies. A week alongside was also an opportunity to conduct Baptism interviews and to carry out baptism services on Sunday.

Whilst in harbour there were also a lot of visitors ranging from Admirals to sea cadets. *Invincible* was a very busy ship.

On Monday 11 February we sailed for Portland and entered the harbour on 18th and would be in the hands of the staff of Flag Officer Sea Training (FOST). They, the staff, were going to put the ship through a rigorous series of tests to ensure that the ship's company were, in all respects, ready to take the ship wherever it needed to be.

That Friday there was a fire exercise planned. Fire exercises are hugely important because fighting fires on board a ship is fraught with dangers and problems because of all the different compartments and it's easy for hoses to get snagged and smoke to build up. The fire service is always ready to take part in such exercises in conjunction with our own people and there would be casualty evacuation training as well.

We sailed from Portland on the Monday morning but sailed into heavy fog, so much of the planned programme did not happen. That evening the HODs dined together which was very pleasant and a useful experience for me, in that I got to know them that much more quickly.

During the next few days we were put through our paces, which meant we had early starts and often late finishes with Action Stations at 0700 and Action Stations remaining in place for most of the forenoon. Being at Action Stations meant that all compartments in the ship were sealed off and all watertight doors were closed. To move around the ship was very difficult as all the clips on the doors had to be knocked off and then remade when you had passed through. Everyone wore 'action working dress' which meant three layers of cotton material, that is, cotton underwear, cotton shirt and trousers (working rig) and overalls. The head and face are covered by an anti-flash hood and hand and arms are covered by long anti-flash gauntlets. I also wore a surcoat which had a Cross on the back and 'Bish' written underneath it. Some of the time was spent wearing respirators which made communication difficult but people had to get used to being in these circumstances because that's what we might have to face.

To ensure that the message about dressing correctly got home, a random check took place when several ratings were told to undress. Most were fine but a few clever souls thought they could get away with it and under their overalls were wearing only underpants. They were made to run around the upper deck in their 'smalls'. There were also a few Wrens discovered wearing just bra and pants under their overalls but, of course, they were not made to run around the upper deck! Which did not go down well with the lads. One rule for one…

The reason for the dress 'code' is that three layers gives greater protection in a fire and the use of cotton rather that nylon is that man-made fibres will melt onto the skin and cause a greater degree of burning.

Every time we went to Action Stations everything had to be secured including cabins and messes and areas like the chapel. I and one of the 'schoolies' on board were responsible for securing the chapel which meant all the chairs and all the desks had to be pushed to the back of the compartment and roped together and to the bulkhead. So that in the event of an explosion they don't fly around and become an even greater hazard to the ship and its people. It took time to do that and it took time to undo that, so Action Stations was a very busy time interspersed with long periods of inactivity My Action Stations, if it had happened for real, was of a roving kind. I would move around the ship helping where necessary, usually with any casualties but also to encourage and support.

During these series of exercises however, I worked with Sick Bay. I ran a casualty station down aft in the Wardroom where 'casualties' sustained at the back end of the ship were brought and logged. We kept in close touch with the Sick Bay to ensure that they were fully informed of the number of casualties, the treatment given and to ensure that they could check in to ensure that the level of first aid was property administered. In the event of having to abandon ship we would have to get the casualties up to the quarter deck for evacuation, so knowing who was there was important.

Our final day at Portland was on 7 March, 'call the hands' was at 0515 and this time I stayed in the Sick Bay and made myself useful. The ship was awarded a 'satisfactory' pass from FOST staff, which was very well earned; to receive a 'satisfactory' you have to work very hard. To celebrate, I went for a 4 mile run across the causeway towards Weymouth and in the evening I had a run ashore with the 'medics'. We sailed early the next day, mainly due to the deteriorating weather conditions in the Channel. I think most people were tired and the next phase (10 days) would be just as demanding.

These couple of days were largely uneventful, so I took advantage of the lull and went around the 'parish'. During my perambulations I called at the cobblers to order a pair of mess boots. These are boots that come up to mid-calf, made of soft leather and highly polished, and are worn with a Mess undress uniform. They were made by the Chinese cobbler who lived and worked on board. It was not widely known but the laundries in ships of the Royal Navy were run in my day, by Chinese gentlemen who were employed by an agency in Hong Kong.

This arrangement had been in place for years and years. These gentlemen kept themselves to themselves, they were at liberty to eat in the dining halls and sleep on Mess decks but chose not to. They prepared their own food and slept where they worked. Anyway, I went to the Cobbler's Shop, a small compartment deep in the ship where the cobbler squatted on his bench, working away. I went in and said 'Good morning, I'd like to order a pair of Mess boots and a pair of sandals, please'. 'Yuh', he replied and got a piece of paper, told me to take off my shoes and place my feet, one at a time, on the paper. He then drew around my feet and that was that. I asked when would be ready and was told 'Thursday', two days hence! I said, 'OK, and how much will they cost?' 'Forty pounds.' 'Really?' says I, 'Yuh', he said. So on Thursday I went down and tried the boots on and they fitted perfectly. I still have them and they still fit perfectly, the sandals too. The cobbler on board was not the greatest conversationalist but an incredible worker.

During this time I went with the senior engineer on a tour of the machinery spaces which was really interesting. We climbed so many ladders my legs were aching, we even went up inside the 'uptakes' (funnels). It was a really interesting journey discovering the inner mechanisms of the ship.

The following day was largely uneventful except for a tricky incident on the flight deck when a Sea King helicopter lost a wheel without which it couldn't land. So my friend, 'Kit' Davidson, the senior Air Engineer, who is a very tall man and built like a 'brick outhouse' went out onto the flight deck. The helicopter came down, hovering about eight feet above the deck, and Kit attached the new wheel while the pilot was trying to keep the helicopter steady above him. The 'downdraft' must have been incredible but he did it nonetheless. I was very impressed.

We went to Action Stations the next morning at 0800 and would remain at in this state until the following Tuesday. I presented the evenings TV entertainment in full action dress but not respirator! It was very uncomfortable and hot but we were told to expect to be attacked at any time. After a while I felt 'grubby' and was very tired due to lack of sleep, as did we all.

On Sunday I was able to hold the 0800 service but the chapel had to be secured afterwards.

The 1000 service was put back until there was a 'window' at 1630 and the Captain gave the go ahead. So, 'action' church was hastily rigged in the JRDH. It was the usual hymn/prayer type with hymns played by the ship's band and sung lustily. There were about 60 souls gathered, including the Captain who always led from the front and was a great supporter. The shortened Holy Communion which followed saw around a dozen communicants, as so many had to return to their station. I was grateful that, under extremely busy circumstances, the Day of Resurrection was observed. An hour or so later we were stood down and were able to relax and have an evening meal and a shower.

Next morning we were promised very bad weather. The 'rattlers' went at 0900, we were at 'action stations' until lunch time and we were inundated with casualties hitting us hard to the last minute. But nothing lasts forever and at mid-day the Admiral came on board and declared an 'End Ex'. This was followed by a 'clear lower deck' when the ship's company was addressed by the Captain and the ship got back to normal. The church/schoolroom was cleaned and set out as usual. My cabin was unsecured and I restored the parrot to his place. Sometime before, my children bought me a toy parrot. He came with me when I was on board and resided in my cabin. I would talk to him –he was a constant companion.

One of the new skills I learnt whilst on board was painting ships crests in the 'chippy's' shop. Ship's crests are quite unique, each ship has its own unique badge and whenever we were on good will visits it's one of the things the Captain presents to visiting dignitaries or to those he calls on, as mementos of our time with them. As a result, there had to be quite a lot of them in store because you can give away quite a lot in just one visit. Each ship has a special plaster cast and the plaster is mixed, poured into the mould and allowed to set. It is then painted and stuck to a wooden backing, hence the 'chippy' being in charge of them. I found it to be a very therapeutic and enjoyable time. It was always a talking point and an opportunity to speak to people I even persuaded the Captain to join in on one occasion and that was a talking point!

That evening we had the first meeting of the Entertainment Committee, after which it was declared a 'Saturday Night at Sea', coupled with a delayed St.

Patrick's Night and it all became very jolly. The weather turned awful. From mid-day we had 70 km winds blowing which, in an aircraft carrier makes it move around quite a lot. We were due in Portsmouth the following afternoon and we came alongside at 1515 as planned. It had been a very interesting few weeks and without doubt the ship's company had gelled.

On 3 April we sailed at 1000 in Procedure Alpha. It was a sunny day but cold and windy. There were lots of people on the Round Tower at the entrance to Portsmouth Harbour to see us off. We had word that two of our aircraft were slightly broken but would be quickly repaired. We continued our passage towards Plymouth and then halfway down the English Channel we had to turn and sprint back up to Portsmouth to recover the aircraft. We achieved a speed of 28 knots (around 32 miles an hour, not bad for a 20000 ton ship). The weather was getting worse but the aircraft were recovered and we were on our way, 18 hours behind schedule. The wind had reached Gale Force 7-8. It was like a ghost ship, as a great number of my shipmates had been struck down with 'mal de mere'.

It was to be a long, long night; the weather was dreadful, we sustained damage to one of the 'Goalkeeper' close point defence systems, which had been hit by baulks of timber. It was thought that perhaps a freighter had shed some of its load and that we ran over this flotsam, which crashed into several parts of the ship not only on the upper deck but also underneath. When one of the sonar operators opened up the compartment the following morning it was flooded, so the dome which covered the equipment underwater must have been damaged. The timber must have been sucked under the ship. Fortunately there was no damage to the propellers or shafts. The after berthing bay, where the Captain's barge was secured, had been struck and though the barge had not been wrecked, it needed a lot of work to put it to rights. The plans for sports/barbecue had to be put back from Sunday to Wednesday.

In a conversation with the Captain before leave, he'd asked that some form of entertainment be thought up in order to get the entire ship's company together, so we came up with the idea of a sports afternoon followed by a BBQ and horse racing evening. The 'horse racing' is held on a 'course'. A long strip of canvas was divided into painted sections and there would be six horses of different colours. There were two dice and two buckets, one of the dice had each face painted a different colour corresponding to the colours of the horses and the other dice had the usual numbered dots. To play, the first dice with the colours on it would be thrown and then the numbered dice would be thrown. If the throw was red and three, then the red horse moved forward three sections. To win, a horse had to cross the line with the exact number, so if you were scored six and only need two then you went forward two sections and back four. Simple! The complicated stuff was the Tote and that was worked out by sharper minds than mine. I never did get the hang of it.

On Wednesday afternoon after lunch we began to prepare for the upper deck sports and barbecue and horse racing. The sports included deck hockey, a deck football with a manufactured ball as it is too expensive to use proper footballs. They kept disappearing over the side! There was also deck 'cricket' which was great and then in in the late afternoon we began the evening activities of horse racing on the flight deck. The Chief's mess had, at my request, dug out a very large barbecue drum made out of oil drums cut in half lengthways, cleaned, and rested on removable legs. The BBQ was already 'flashed up' and the 'can man' had set up his bar with a good stock of cans.

The sailors and marines were allowed two cans per day. I thought that we had arranged for them to have their own daily allowance on deck rather than in their messes. . I assumed that that was what the NAAFI manager was doing. How wrong I was. I discovered that the 'can man', instead of sticking to the two cans rule, got rid of his stock quickly with the result that, though it wasn't exactly drunkenness, there was an awful lot of people in a merry state.

Inevitably there were many arrests for 'lip locking' and other attempts at lovemaking all over the upper deck as the 'No touching' rules was broken on a massive scale. However, it could have been worse had things been allowed to continue. The Commander wanted to pipe 'Clear the flight deck' but the Captain ever wise, ordered the Officer of the Watch to turn the wheel a couple of points and in easy stages allowed a howling gale to deter the amorous adventures from going further. Things just got out of hand. 'Kit' Davidson came to me and said 'Come and have a look at this', so we walked aft and looked down into the 'Goalkeeper' sponson (the gun emplacement) only to see a mattress. 'I think someone is going to try to nest tonight', he said, 'what should we do about it? 'Well, we could heave it over the side or stow it away somewhere', I said. So the mattress was removed.

The following morning, I happened to be in the Regulating Office having a cup of tea with the Master-at-Arms when a young sailor came in and said 'Excuse me, Master, I've come to report the loss of a mattress'. Every head turned to him. 'Come inside' the Master at Arms said, 'we've been waiting for you'. He got 'weighed off' for the cost of the mattress and he was given a severe dressing down for his intentions.

The aftermath of the evening meant that the Commander's Table was very busy over the next few days and a lot of people would not be going ashore in Norfolk. More dangerous still was the state of the flight deck. Prior to flying, a minute search is made of the flight deck to remove any debris or rubbish, no matter how small, because even the smallest item if sucked into the air intakes of a Harrier could destroy it or cause it to crash. So a line of sailors moved along the deck, picking up anything that should not be there.

Imagine their surprise when a very sleepy sailor was

found in the netting under the bows, 60 feet above the sea. The idiot could have been killed. The litter all along the deck was dreadful and the Flight Deck Officer was incandescent with rage because the flight deck looked like the aftermath of a pop concert. Flying was delayed but it could have been much worse. It was something which was bound to happen. If you put young men and young women together in a hull and send them thousands of miles away from home they are going to do exactly what young people have been doing for millions of years or try to! Eventually, this event got to the Press and *Invincible* was deemed 'The Love Boat', which did not please the Captain one iota.

Once the weather eased, divers went down to examine the sonar dome and found it smashed. It would need a dry dock repair when we got to Norfolk, Virginia so a signal was sent requesting this. Putting divers in the water to check the hull is always difficult as an aircraft carrier's upper works acts like a sail. So even with engines stopped the slightest breeze can push her through the water at walking pace. However, they did it. To their astonishment a very large turtle suddenly appeared alongside them, slowly making its way to Africa. A 'pipe' was made and soon a very great number of people were gazing down from the ship's side at this wonderful creature who, apart from wondering why a grey wall was in the middle of the ocean, completely ignored us and carried on his or hers sedate way. What a lovely sight.

We arrived in Norfolk Virginia on the 5 April and

shifted into whites, that is the white tropical uniform of the Royal Navy. We entered harbour in Procedure Alpha. It was freezing! Norfolk Naval Base is huge, it's about 17 miles from one side to the other and filled with all kinds of naval hardware.

One of the things that struck me when watching the arrival of the USS *America* was the sheer size of some of the American ships. *Invincible,* a 20,000 aircraft carrier was the capital ship of the Royal Navy but all around us were these huge 90,000 aircraft carriers of the United States Navy.

We sailed on 20 April at 0730 and went to action stations at 0930. We would be exercising with units of the American fleet for the next two weeks and it was a very busy time. We also entertained a number of Americans one evening. They had landed their helicopter on board, but it developed a fault and they couldn't take off, so they enjoyed our hospitality. American ships are dry and therefore they liked our beer.

On the Tuesday I spent the day with the flight deck crew. I got dressed in overalls and had a tour of one of the hangers and flight deck. They explained what equipment they used and I worked with them, as best I could, throughout the day as there was a full flying programme. In the afternoon I was asked if I would like to launch a Harrier and I said, 'Yes please' and they gave me instructions. The flight deck officer said, 'Whatever you do remember you've got to get down low because the back wash from the aircraft is quite strong'. I watched them during the next couple of launches, practiced a bit until I said 'OK'. I was ready to go. I indicated to the pilot that I would be his 'launcher', I looked up at the island and when I got three green lights I waved my little flags and pointed to the bows and the aircraft began to roll. I dropped down to the deck with one leg stretched out in front of me and the other behind (as close to the 'splits' as I could get) but I didn't drop down far enough. The back wash came up underneath me, scooped me up and I tumbled along the flight deck like tumbleweed in a western film. I wasn't hurt, I had a couple scratches but I felt a complete prat! Everybody was falling about laughing at my antics but I became great friends with the flight deck crew.

Quite a lot was happening on the ship's TV. We had started a programme called 'Saint and Greasy', which mirrored the sports programme 'The Saint and Greavsie' on ITV at that time. One of the Education Officers dressed up in a leather jacket and slicked back his hair and I was 'The Saint' (type cast again!). The engineers manufactured a halo for me, which went down the back of my shirt, and we had the same fast talking double act as the ITV show.

We arrived in Barbados in Procedure Alpha at 0630 on Saturday 4 May. The ship's company had now been at sea for several weeks, including two weeks of working hard with the Americans. They deserved a break and Barbados was it.

The following Sunday about eight of us went to Saint

Michael's Cathedral in Bridgetown for the 0900 Eucharist. There were about 400 communicants which was fabulous. All the ladies wore hats and colourful dress. It was really excellent and the people made such a fuss of us; we could not have wished for a better welcome.

The Roman Catholic chaplain, Richard Madders had joined the ship and would be with us for our homeward trip. I introduced him to number of people and explained the layout of the chapel/vestry and sorted out the times for Mass with him.

We sailed from Barbados on Saturday 11 May at 0615. I spent the day showing Richard around. We both had to prepare for Sunday so we talked at length about his role on board. As far as I was concerned it was a 50/50 situation, he could share the television and the radio too but all I asked was that we kept each other informed as to where we were going in terms of mess deck visiting. What I didn't want to happen was me arriving at the mess deck if Richard was already there or vice versa. Late on in the afternoon the CO of 814 Squadron came to see me and said that, after much thought, he would like to be Confirmed. I was delighted and outlined to him the kind of confirmation preparations that would be required for him and how we would manage the instruction.

The clocks went back and the weather got colder. We entered the English Channel on 21 May arriving in Portsmouth the following day, getting alongside at 1600.

Having returned from the western Atlantic deployment, the ship was to be in harbour until the end of August. During the months of June, July and August the ship underwent a great deal of maintenance and preparation for the next deployment. However, the normal routines carried on, including a number of welfare committee meetings. These were important as far as the ship's company were concerned as we looked at the ship's company dance, sporting fixtures and discussed the next deployment; anything, in fact, that affected the people.

As part of the overall maintenance schedule it been planned that the ship would move into dry dock so that the sonar dome could be replaced and other maintenance below the water line could be carried out. Temporary repairs to the dome had been carried out in America but the dome needed to be replaced. Once in dry dock the ship would be largely uninhabitable so the ship's company had to move into barracks in *HMS Nelson,* my old parish.

We would report on board each morning and work as normal until secure. Then the only people on board were the duty watch. It was quite extraordinary being in the ship when it moved into dry dock. It is an elaborate procedure but very skilfully carried out by the dockyard 'mateys'.

Once the ship was secure and the dock empty and relatively dry, we took a stroll under the ship. We had hard hats on of course, but if a 20,000 ton aircraft carrier dropped on your head, hard hats wouldn't save you from having a headache! That weekend I took John under the ship. He was really impressed and not a little apprehensive. I did suggest to the welfare committee that we hold a barbecue under the ship and raise money for 'King George V Fund for Sailors', Captain Tolhurst agreed but the dockyard authorities refused our request on the grounds of health and safety.

The ship was duly re-floated and just before leave I had a visit in my cabin from a Leading Hand of one of the Seaman's messes. He told me that he was very concerned about one of his mess mates and would I speak with him? I asked what he was concerned about and he told me that this lad, fresh out of *Raleigh,* had taken to wandering the dockyard in the early hours and when the ship was in dry dock he would spend time staring down into the dock. Later that day I had a visit from the killick's divisional officer who expressed the same concerns. I pointed out that, though I would be very happy to see the young man, it would have to come from him, I cannot make him talk to me. Next day there was a knock on my door and there was this very large young man, tall and broad with a ruddy complexion. 'Come in, would you like a cup of tea?' I asked. 'Yes please, Bish'. He replied with a Midlands accent. I asked him his name and he replied, 'Tom, Tom Cobbley'. I asked what was troubling him and said 'I hate ships, I feel all enclosed, so in a tiny bunk I feel as if I'm being squashed so I have to get up and go for a walk'. I asked why he was staring into the dry dock already knowing the answer. He said, 'It would be a quick way out'. 'How many ships have you served in?' I asked, 'This is my first'. 'Well, if you are claustrophobic in this one what will you be like in a minesweeper?' 'I dread to think', he said. 'But why did you join the Navy?' His reply revealed all. It transpired that he was born in Leicestershire and, not being a great student, left school at 15and a half and went to work on a farm. He loved it. However, his father, who had been in the Army and his brother who served with the Parachute Regiment, used to tease him about his dead-end job and how it wasn't a proper job for a man. Their comments and his desire to please had led him to join the Navy.

I asked if he had spoken to our doctors on board and he told me that he had and they had offered sleeping tablets. I then asked what he would like to do and he said, 'I'd like to leave'. I said, 'I cannot get you out but I know a man who can. I want you to go and see Surgeon Commander Morgan O'Connell, who is a psychiatrist in Haslar, the Naval hospital at Gosport'. 'I'm not mad,' he said. 'I'm not saying you are', I replied, 'but if you broke your arm you would go and see a doctor who could help, but it's your mind that's bothering you, so you need to see a "mind" doctor'. Reluctantly he agreed.

One of the problems of being on board a ship in harbour is the difficulty in getting a phone line out but on this occasion it all worked perfectly. I picked up the phone in my cabin, asked the exchange to put me through to Haslar and asked their exchange to put me through to Commander O'Connell and the phone was answered instantly. I had known Morgan O'Connell for some time since I attended a Welfare Counselling course at Amport House. His greeting was rude, ' Hello, you old bastard, what can I do for you?' 'That's no way to speak to a priest of the True Church,' I replied and he laughed. I told him of the young man, 'Send him over straight away,' and he put the phone down. I went to the Commander, John Rimington and outlined the problem. 'My fear', I said,' is that once we are back at sea he will take a 'header' over the side'. Transport was arranged and I told Tom, 'When you come back, come straight to me, OK?' With that, one of the Regulators drove him around to Haslar.

Two hours or so later my phone rang and it was Morgan O'Connell who said, 'He has to go right away for he is suicidal. I have given him notes to give to your Commander and onwards. Let me know how it all goes'. Tom came back with the documents and we both went to the Commander who summoned the Master at Arms and told him.

So young Tom gathered his possessions and left the ship for *Nelson* and eventual discharge without a blemish on his character. I said to him as we parted on the gangway, 'Go and drive your tractor and be happy. As for your father and brother, tell them to, 'F….off'. When our sick bay found out that Tom had gone they were not best pleased at 'my interference' as they put it, and I said, 'He came to you and you offered him pills'.

Main leave finished on 19 August and preparations

were made for sailing for our next deployment to the Mediterranean. First, came a 'work up' with the squadrons in the Moray Firth, on the east coast of Scotland. This work up had to be planned, so the usual departmental meetings ensued.

There was about 30% change in the ship's complement and within the squadrons, so working up was vital to ensure the efficiency and wellbeing of the ship. There were a lot of people trying to find their way around the ship in those early days, some were simply lost or needing directions and I sympathized because I could remember my first days on board.

We had one week to prepare for the work up. It's not just the ship's company that needed to get used to one another but the squadrons had to do so as well. There had been changes in the flight deck crew and the aircraft maintenance teams. The squadrons needed time in the air to practice tactics and whatever evolutions needed to be done. The open waters of the Moray Firth were ideal.

A great deal of work had to be done as we were proceeding from work up to a major exercise with other NATO Navies in Norwegian waters within the Arctic Circle. The exercise was titled 'Teamwork' but we'll come to that in due course. From the Arctic Circle we were to sail around the top of Scotland through the Irish Sea, out into the Western Approaches and on to Lisbon and the Mediterranean. We would not be coming back to Portsmouth or touching at any other port, so whatever we needed to take with us had to be brought on board during the next seven days. From my perspective there were a number of things that had to be done. There were wreaths to be brought on board all of which had to be biodegradable. I don't know why it happens, but the ship's programme had been released to local papers and someone in the Royal British Legion branch at Hayling Island saw that we were putting into Alexandria. He telephoned the ship and was naturally put through to me. The enquiry was to ask if there were plans to visit the memorial at El Alamein and, if so, would we lay a wreath on behalf of the 8th Army Veterans Association which has its headquarters at Hayling Island. I agreed and went out to see the people at Hayling Island where I found that they were the first Legion branch to be created in 1921. A very nice club and very nice people, so I was happy to help them.

Anyway, I collected the wreaths and brought them on board. Other preparations included liaising with the management of the '5th Avenue Club' on the arrangements for the ship's company dance to be held later that year; collect the dance ticket and raffle tickets and buy quiz books ready for the Thursday night quizzes. These had not been all that well attended, so there was to be a big push through the Welfare Committee to promote them.

I had also tried get the addresses of clergy in the ports that we would be visiting so that I could visit them and pay due respects, as it were. In addition, I had to ensure that the vestry was well stocked. The day before we sailed there were a few baptisms to conduct by myself and the Roman Catholic chaplain, so the quarterdeck and Chapel were quite busy.

On 27 August we sailed in Procedure Alpha and quite a lot of families were on the Round Tower. We reached the Moray Firth and the training began. There was an NBCD exercise for the entire ship's company which lasted the whole day, increasing in difficulty as it progressed.

It was important that everybody knew what they had to do and where they were supposed to be. We were flying constantly, as the aircraft had to 'work up' together and with the ship.

Day-to-day activities outside of exercises were the usual combination of mess deck visiting, running the TV and radio studio, appearing on television, running the quizzes and being part of welfare committee meetings. There were the daily Command Briefs and HODs meetings which all made for a very busy schedule. Planning services went on in the same way. The departments that were to sponsor church were contacted early in the week so that they could select the hymns and readers. A few days later the band were given the hymns so they could practice; nothing had changed from previous deployments and that was a standard weekly routine.

On 10 September, the day began with drama. At 0545 a helicopter 'ditched' and the ship proceeded towards it. Eventually, we reached the helicopter, which was floating nicely on a very flat, calm sea, its floatation bags had gone off and the air crew were waving to us from the doorway. It was craned back on board and no harm was done. We were lucky because that evening the weather turned cold and stormy.

The weather deteriorated once we sailed from the Moray Firth and remained awful for the next few days. There was no flying because the parameters of flying depended on the pitch and roll of the flight deck and given the sea state there was no way aircraft could be launched. Everybody was tired because the constant motion of the ship made sleeping difficult.

The interesting thing was that the Americans, the Norwegians and the other ships moved into the fjords to give their ship's companies some rest but everybody knows 'Britannia rules the waves' so we stayed out. *HMS Newcastle*, one of our escorts, sustained real casualties. They had three sailors injured, one with a broken arm, another with cracked ribs and another with a dislocated shoulder. They could not be brought across to our hospital because of the sea state. As I say, everybody was very tired but the weather calmed as we crossed into the Arctic Circle and the flying parameters came back in bounds. But an incident took place on the flight deck as they wound up the 'Harriers' for launching. A young aircraft handler stood too close to the air intakes. Now, the 'Harrier' was an extremely greedy aircraft and this young man was lifted off his feet by the air going into the engine and could have been chopped up by the fans. But what happened was that the strap on his helmet broke and the helmet went into the engine. This gave the aircraft a severe dose of indigestion whilst he sustained severe bruising to the throat and larynx.

I heard the pipe 'Standing First Aid Party close up' and went to the sick bay to find out how he was. On my way back I bumped into the Admiral and he asked how the sailor was. I said, 'No thanks to you Sir, he will be fine'. 'What do you mean?' he said. 'How long has this exercise been planned one, two years?' I asked. 'Something like that'. 'Well, couldn't the plans have included a weekend break, everyone is tired?' 'You were just worried about church services,' he said and then I lost my temper and said, 'You think I'm only concerned about church services? That young man made a mistake because he was tired, he could have been killed and it's not you that would bury him, it would be me and I would have to comfort his parents, not you.' 'It's a very busy exercise period'. 'Yes sir', I replied, 'exercise, not war. If the others took a weekend off, why couldn't we?' The admiral didn't say anything, he just 'Harrumphed' and walked off.

A red mist had descended. I stormed back to my cabin and slammed the door. A minute or so later and my phone rang, it was the Captain, 'Come up and see me,' he said, so I climbed the seven decks up to the Captain's sea cabin on the island. 'Come in and close the door.' I thought I was going to get a severe 'bollocking' about something. He said, 'How did you get away with it?' 'Sorry sir, with what?' 'That bollocking you gave the admiral, I have wanted to do that for a long time, well done!' Puzzled, I asked, 'How do you know about that, it's just happened?' Apparently, the dinner queue was forming behind me but I hadn't realised it. I also did not know that the 'jungle drums' worked that fast!

The Admiral never spoke to me again.

Having crossed into the Arctic Circle it meant that we were all issued with 'Blue Nose' certificates to prove that we had been there. The exercises were successful and we learned a great deal about working with other ships and aircraft. By the time it was all over the ships company had gelled.

'Teamwork' ended on 19 September and the Admiral and his staff departed the following day. Then began our voyage around the north of Scotland, down the Irish Sea and out into the Western Approaches, heading for Lisbon.

A couple of things happened on our way down to Lisbon. First, it was the mail or lack of it. People don't seem to understand how important mail was to sailors, even if it was two or three weeks late, it didn't matter and when it arrived the morale of the ship lifted perceptibly. We knew that there were sacks of mail waiting for us at RAF Prestwick and we asked if one of their helicopters could drop them off to us as we passed. Although they didn't refuse, they made every excuse under the sun.

In the end we dispatched one of our 'Sea Kings' with a regulator, to go and collect the mail. When they got there, there was complete indifference. It was a case of the RAF playing 'silly beggars' and in the end our men were told where it was and went and fetched it themselves. In retaliation the helicopter crew pinched the pennant off the Station Commander's car; he was a Group Captain and very grand!

Not long after the helicopter retuned Captain John received a very 'snotty' signal demanding the return of the pennant and dire consequences to those who had stolen it. Our Captain rolled his eyes heavenward and said, 'Well, give it back to him. They really are silly,' and it was duly returned but by a roundabout way. I think it was posted third class from Gibraltar or was it Istanbul? No matter, that's the RAF for you!

The second thing that happened was the high seas firing in the Western Approaches. The weather had abated and we were able to launch the missiles successfully, which proved the system worked. We proceeded on our way and arrived in Lisbon on 27 September. Lisbon is a beautiful city which I have visited on a number of occasions and my admiration for the city has not diminished. Having obtained the addresses and telephone numbers of the chaplains of the ports that we were to visit I got in touch with the chaplain of the Anglican church in Lisbon whose name was Ken Robinson. He proved to be a delightful man who kindly invited me to preside at the Harvest Eucharist in the church at Estoril, a seaside town.

On Sunday morning transport was available to take about twelve of us to the church at Estoril. Having obtained directions, we arrived outside the church but it was like no church I had ever seen. It was a tall door set between the fire station on one side and a department store on the other. I tried the door and went into a beautiful, modern church built in circular form attached to the rear of the buildings either side. A large congregation welcomed us and the really lovely service followed, after which there was a Harvest lunch, which was delightful. Their hospitality was almost overwhelming. We sailed from Lisbon on 1 October, 'Call the Hands' was at 0600 and we sailed at 0730 for the Straights of Gibraltar and the Mediterranean.

Over the next few days the routines of the ship were exactly the same as they had been before, with the exception of two new services that I introduced now that we were in the Mediterranean and the weather was better. Quarter Deck Prayers took place twice a week on Tuesday and Thursday at 0750 before the working day commenced and depending on the ship's programme. Sometimes we would have half a dozen, sometimes none depending on what the ship was doing but it was such a lovely way to start the day, looking out at the sunshine on a Mediterranean morning and offering that day to God in prayer. The other thing I did was to introduce a Bible study group. This took place in the evening once a week and it had a very mixed attendance but it was worth doing, if only to see the worship of the Lord advertised on Daily Orders.

That afternoon we came to anchor three miles off the

Egyptian coast as our next port of call was Alexandria. The following morning those of us who were going to Alamein left the ship at 0830 and descended the side ladder onto a platform called a 'cat' from where boats took us into the harbour. Buses took us to El Alamein, the site of the famous battle of the Second World War. The sight was quite breath taking – as far as the eye could see were the headstones of those who had died at that battle, the German and Italian war memorials were quite impressive but nothing took our breath away like the site of all of those graves.

There were about 50 of us in the coach, all young men and women, and they were struck to silence. I reminded them before we left the coach that all the graves they would see would be memorials to young people about their ages doing a task that enabled us to live in freedom. It was, I think, a timely reminder. We returned to Alexandria for lunch and a swim in the Mediterranean but there was a melancholy mood throughout. The sight of that cemetery would live with us for a very long time.

When we got back, the 'cat' had been removed and we had to go up a 'jumping' ladder (a rope ladder with wooden rungs) which was very hair-raising. The weather has got slightly worse and the ship was rolling around, so if you got your hands in the wrong place your fingers could be crushed against the ship's side but we all made it up safely. It was perhaps an appropriate end to a very disconcerting day.

The following day, 20 October was a Sunday and the

date closest to the battle of El Alamein. Some of us were going back to El Alamein but this time to attend the international memorial service and to lay the wreaths that we had brought. We were also providing a guard of honour as the UK Defence Minister, Mr Soames, would be representing the government.

My alarm went off at 0500 for an early breakfast and once again there was a boat transfer. So another scramble down the jumping ladders but this time we went in civilian clothes and our uniforms were in clothes bags to keep them clean. Driving through the desert on a straight road that looks like a black ribbon stretching out in front with the scrub desert either side was very atmospheric.

We stopped and changed and John Carson, the 'schoolie' who was the other half of our TV show 'The Saint and Greasy', was to present a wreath on behalf of the ship whilst I was presenting one on behalf of the 8th Army Veterans. There was a large crowd gathered, this being an international service of memorial, we presented the wreaths and had photographs taken in order that I might show them to the Association members at Hayling Island. Once the service was over we returned to *Fort Grange,* the Fleet Auxiliary for lunch and to await *Invincibe's* arrival at 1700.

The amazing thing was that the Egyptian Port Authority did not have a gangway long enough to reach from the dockside to the ship so they lashed two together, which was very much a 'Heath Robinson' affair. It bounced alarmingly when anyone walked over it. But it didn't collapse so no one fell in the water.

The following afternoon I watched the ship's football team play *Edinburgh*, one of our escort ships. We lost 4-1. I wasn't impressed. What irritated me was that their team members arrived by minibus, climbed out smoking and had had a run ashore the night before and so were hung over. No, I wasn't impressed. I left early because one of the lads was hurt and I took him back to the ship.

Later I went into town to buy prizes for the ship's company quiz. This was interesting, as I had to haggle with the shopkeepers. The welfare committee on the run up the Mediterranean decided that the quiz prizes would reflect the visits that we made, so in Lisbon we bought bottles of white port and in Alexandria I bought a number of fezzes and things particularly Egyptian. The winning mess would be able to raffle the prizes amongst the mess members if they wished. Next day there was a coach trip to Cairo. We left at 0800 for a three hour journey. We went straight to the museum and then on to the Pyramids of Giza via a papyrus factory

Going inside the pyramid was an interesting experience. A long, low tunnel led into the empty central chamber. It was very hot and crowded and if there was any hint of claustrophobia it was wise to stay outside. The surface of the pyramids was very badly worn, which is to be expected really. Not far away a man was offering camel rides at a price. I went on a camel ride after re-arranging the price.

The following day we went to Memphis which was

rather disappointing and then on to Saqqara and the Pyramid of Eunice. But when you've seen one pyramid, you've seen them all! Next came a visit to a carpet factory which we thought quite disgraceful. The sailors got really angry because the people making carpets were children and our guide was protesting that this was an important part of their family's income but, nevertheless, our guide had a bit of an 'ear bashing, from the sailors.

We were joined on Saturday by Admiral 'Jock' Slater, a delightful man and a sailor of the 'old school'. Once he and his staff were on board, we sailed on the next leg of our deployment. The Trafalgar Night Dinner had been delayed to accommodate the Admiral. He was grateful for that as he could not remember the last time he had attended a Trafalgar Night dinner at sea.

While transiting the Sea of Marmara we passed the Gallipoli Memorial and lots of our people took the opportunity to photograph this very sombre sight. With the Captain's permission, I gave a short explanation over the main broadcast as to the Gallipoli landings, its background and the results of the campaign.

On the Thursday night there was a distress call that came to us from a ship called the MV *Hawk*, five people from Swansea, of all places, were on board. One little girl had a broken leg and there was a handicapped boy. They seemed a very strange group of people in a very odd craft which had lost all power. The weather was quite blustery and the sea was very choppy so, with some difficulty, our deputy engineer was flown across to them and sent down by winch, which again was quite was quite difficult because the wind was blowing him about and he was swinging back-and-forth. But they got him down as close as they could and at the appropriate moment he pressed the button and dropped onto the deck. If he mis-timed it, he would have ended up in the sea but he didn't. In any event he couldn't start the engines so we had to take the vessel in tow and bring the people on board. They did not seem particularly grateful for our help and expected to have everything they wanted, including children's clothing! We brought them safely into our next port of call, Palermo in Sicily.

A number of other people would be flying home from Sicily or moving on to other appointments or courses. One of them was my colleague in the television studio, John Carson who played the part of 'Greasy'. I would have to continue as the 'Saint' on my own. Those who were leaving were dined out that night. The weather changed, it was beautiful and Palermo, surrounded by hills was an absolute delight. In the afternoon I went for a walk and located the Anglican Church, a part of the Diocese of Europe but sadly the church itself was not open. So I telephoned the chaplain who told me that the church had been closed for renovation but was opening the following day for the first time for several months. Re-dedication was to be conducted by the Archdeacon of Florence. He invited us to attend and when I got back to the ship I put the word around and a goodly number attended, including the Captain.

An interesting service in more ways than one because I had a proposal of marriage after the service. The lady sitting in front of us thought that my singing voice was worthy of marriage. I had to explain to her that I was already married and that unfortunately, having a singing voice is not really the best reason for getting married, however she was a very attractive woman!

That afternoon a number of us went to see Palermo play another football team in Division Two of the Italian League. It was interesting to watch the Italians in all their glory. They are so clothes-conscious that even going to football match was a fashion statement. We were in jeans and top coats but they were in these wonderful suits and tailored overcoats. I don't remember the score but one of our people had his wallet, ID card and tickets pickpocketed. There was not much we could do about it. We clubbed together to buy him another ticket and reported the theft to the police. That didn't do much good either. Previous experience caused me to put my money and ID card in my sock.

Next morning we had breakfast at 0630 as there was a coach trip to Mount Etna. We arrived at 1230 after a very pleasant journey, watching the Sicilian country side as we drove along. The climb was tiring. The crater was smoking quietly so we couldn't venture inside, only to the rim, then it was back on the coach for the long journey back.

We stopped in a small town where there was a toy shop and I bought several shotguns. Sicily and shotguns go together, well, they did in 'The Godfather'. I had not been in my cabin long when there was a knock on the door and it was the Master at Arms, 'Excuse me, Bish, but I have been told that you brought shotguns on board. I have to remind you that bringing firearms on board can only be done with permission and they have to be stored in my locked cabinets.' 'Absolutely, Master, by all means confiscate them' I said, and opened my prizes drawer and there were the toy shotguns, complete with corks in the barrels. He looked at me and said, 'I am going to kill the little sod who told me. I'll teach him to wind me up!' 'Never mind,' says I, 'come in and have a dram'. Which he did.

We sailed the following morning at 0930 and moved into the usual routines at sea. I'm very glad that I started Quarterdeck prayers because although the numbers were never great, those who did come found it very helpful and of course it's always good see it in Daily Orders.

The following Sunday, 10 November was Remembrance Sunday. The early Communion was followed at 1030 with the Remembrance Day Service on the flight deck. It was a beautiful day and it all went very well, considering that the boys and girls hadn't done any parade training for a long time. The bulk of the ship's company was there and the Captain presented wreaths which were laid on the sea. It was a very memorable service.

That evening just to remind us that aircraft carriers are dangerous places, there was an incident on the flight deck when a Harrier on a night flying exercise landed on top of another one. Its tail landed on the nose of a parked aircraft. Although not much damage was done the pilot was quite anxious, understandably. All I said to him was

'Any landing you walk away from is a good landing'.

Next day we arrived at Gibraltar. The big event here, as far as I was concerned, was another 'Sons and Daughters at Sea'. They were due in on a flight at 1530 from Yeovilton and I was able to show John the sights of Gibralter, both during the day and at night. We sailed the following morning and the young people were there on board to witness 'Leaving Harbour'. A whole programme of visits and events was planned for them but as the ship 'nosed' out into the Atlantic the sea state changed and it became a bit 'bumpy'. There were quite a few who suffered from 'mal de mer' and not just the sons and daughters. Next morning, on my parish rounds I asked the 'can' man at the NAAFI where everyone was. 'I'm told about 70% are down with seasickness,' he said. I could believe it, the place was like a ghost ship.

The following morning there was a firefighting equipment demonstration on the Quarter Deck. In the afternoon they were due to visit 814 and 801 squadrons for demonstrations but, sadly, John was the only youngster there. He then went on to the bridge where he took over from the quartermaster and steered the ship for quite some time. I didn't stay and because he was on his own he actually handled the ship while it was recovering aircraft. It was quite a thrill for him.

That night we had the final round of the quiz. There was absolute chaos as I, once again, gave messes that were well behind the chance to catch up, by bringing items to the studio. As ever, it made the last round very exciting not least for the youngsters who were well enough to attend and, in fact, the remainder of the trip back to Portsmouth was filled with entertainment for them.

The weeks following our return were filled with the usual routines of meetings, baptism interviews, conducting baptisms, preparations for the dance and chasing up tickets. We had been in harbour for a week or so when I was stopped as I walked 'the parish' and a young midshipman asked if he could come and see me. We arranged a time and he appeared at my cabin. I asked him what the problem was and he said he thought he had Aids. I asked him why he thought that and he said that he'd been with a prostitute in Sweden in his previous ship only a couple of months before.

I said I thought it highly unlikely but if he was that bothered why not have a test done? He said no he couldn't, he couldn't do it, he couldn't face the sick bay. I said I wasn't sure that the sick bay could do it but anyway, we could arrange for a test to be done in a civilian clinic. I told him I would go with him if he wanted. He reluctantly agreed after I had assured him that I would arrange time off with his 'boss' without giving the real reason. I made a few phone calls and booked an appointment for him for the following afternoon. I went to find him and said, 'I'll pick you up at the gangway at 1300 tomorrow. In the meantime don't have too much to drink tonight as you'll need a clear head tomorrow.'

The following morning I drove to the ship and parked in my 'slot' as usual but I had this feeling that something was wrong. A number of vehicles and people were gathered around the gangway, and when I went up, the duty watch said, 'There's been a death on board Bish,' and I knew exactly what had happened. I went to my cabin, took off my coat and went up onto the main cabin deck but one of the ship's Regulators said to me, 'You can't go any further Bish.' I said, 'I know who it is so would you ask the SIB (Special Investigation Branch) to contact me please? I'll be in my cabin.'

A few minutes later the head investigator of the SIB came down and we sat and I told him about young Kevin. It seems that the lad was determined to end his life. Apparently, after 'Call the Hands' the Duty Steward was taking tea around. She knocked on his door and called, 'Tea, Sir'. When there was no reply she opened the door and found that he had hanged himself. But here was the strange thing, he had tried to hang himself with two ties knotted together, one end around the 'grab' bar on the deck head and the other end around his neck. He jumped off his bunk but the tie snapped. In the end he used belts and strangled himself because his feet were on the deck. I was heartbroken for him and could not imagine the despair that must have been going on in his mind. I was really upset but even more upset for Yvette Thomas, the steward who found him. I went to see her and talked to her but she was fairly resilient and very courageous and was so sad for the lad.

I went to see the Captain and said, 'I thought we'd won this one,' but he said, 'Just so sad, so very sad but at least you tried'. I telephoned the boy's pastor in Scotland and broke the news to him and he too was very greatly upset and told me that since the breakup of his parents' marriage Kevin had become like a twig floating around on the water, not knowing which way to go. It seems that he had no other immediate family members but the pastor would inform his parents and arrangements would be made to take Kevin's body home to Scotland.

The life of the ship went on and the meetings that were held on board all revolved around Christmas leave and the preparations for it, but the HODs meetings were also taken up with details of the deployment scheduled for the following year.

The meeting was chaired on this occasion by the Captain who wanted a report from each of us as to the preparedness of each department. He also wanted activities on board to be overseen by a HOD. So there and then activities and sports were divided up between us. Entertainment fell to Neil and I again, with TV and radio staying with me. No one wanted to oversee the football teams so I volunteered for that. As far as sport was concerned the Captain wanted a winning mentality, so every effort must be made to present the ship in a good 'light'. I asked how much latitude I had as far as the football teams were concerned. 'You can't have them flogged,' was the reply.

I decided to sack the football manager, a Chief Petty Officer who had been in charge for too long. What I witnessed in Egypt meant that there had to be changes given the Captain's directive on winning mentality. I asked to see him and when he came to see me I said, 'Chief, at a recent HODs meeting I was appointed chairman of the football club by the Captain and my first act as chairman is to tell you that you are no longer in charge of the team.' He looked stunned and said, 'You can't do that'. I replied, 'It's done, you are no longer in charge.' I had done some preparatory work after that HODs meeting and approached an officer called Des Evans, a very good footballer in his day and said, 'Des, remember that awful result in Egypt that you were so cross about it?' 'Yes'. 'Well, how would you fancy managing the teams?' 'Yes please,' he replied with a broad grin. It was a done deal before the sacking!

Over the next few days we talked about how he wanted to run the teams and I said we needed to get a team spirit working. To that end I suggested regular 'get togethers' on board and I then contacted a local man who was a Football League referee to come and give us a talk, which he did. We had a good turnout, not only of the existing team members but those who were interested. It was the first of many such meetings prior to and during the deployment. I also thought that we should have our own club shirt. A competition had been run on board as to who could design the best logo for 'Orient 92' and that design would be incorporated onto all aspects of deployment goods and souvenirs, including shirts.

Other sports clubs on board had selected colours already but the football club had never been that united so I selected a lemon shirt with the logo on it and *HMS Invincible Football Club* embroidered around it. It worked splendidly and the lads liked it. Each bought his own but they were subsidised by the Welfare Committee. I still have mine.

Talking of sport, I am not much of a rugby fan but during this period, the Wales rugby team were taking a beating at almost every game and I came in for some 'stick' as a result. On one occasion, whilst we were at sea, Warren Benbow, Commander Air, an absolutely delightful man, saw me late one Saturday afternoon and crowed about the latest defeat that Wales had suffered at the hands of England. I simply smiled and took it in good part.

Later I was in the Wardroom and he came in and said to me, 'You devious clerical bastard. You knew the Captain was Welsh didn't you?' I replied, 'Well, I knew that he had strong connections in Wales. Why?' It seems that Warren had gone 'bouncing' onto the bridge and said 'Well, Sir, we stuffed the bastards'. The Captain was reading reports and looked over the top of his glasses and said, 'Warren by 'bastards' do you mean the Welsh?' 'Yes, we put them to the sword,' and he laughed uproariously. The Captain said, 'You do realise that I was born in

Wales?' Warren's laughter died and he looked greatly embarrassed. Hence his comments to me. Sometimes small victories are worth waiting for!

Naval HQ at Northwood would continue to fine-tune the deployment according to the requirements of the Foreign Office and the countries that we were to visit but we knew it was going to be a Far East deployment and it was going to be called 'Orient Express '92'. We were urged to prepare our departments accordingly for a long seven months deployment. Further details would come our way as soon as they arrived with the command. We were told not to broadcast the deployment too much as details could and would change over the period of time. Things would become clearer after the next exercise which was titled 'Teamwork', which was to take place in the New Year.

The usual pre- Christmas activities took place, drinks in the Warrant Officer's and Chief's mess, the Wardroom lunch and Christmas ball. For most, Christmas leave began on Friday the 20th but not totally for me, as I had the Christmas services to prepare so, on Christmas Eve I went in to set up the chapel ready for the Christmas morning Eucharist. This time I had bought small gifts for the duty watch. Nothing much, only a bag of sweets and chocolates which would brighten their being on Watch on Christmas Day. I went on board for the 1030 Eucharist in the chapel which became so full that extra chairs had to be put out. The Captain and his family were present and there was an impromptu reception for families in the Wardroom, so while the other Heads of Departments went to see their own people, I helped entertain the families until they returned.

Christmas leave ended on 30 January 1992 and a few days later there was a HODs meeting at which more details of the deployment to the Far East were given. On 15 January in the evening we dined out Commander John and Mrs. Rimington. I was sorry to see John go, he was a lovely man and I thoroughly enjoyed serving with him. My main hope was that his relief was as good. There were many questions that I needed answered by the Chaplain of the Fleet, the first being, would I be staying with the ship for the whole of the deployment; how many chaplains were coming with the other ships; who were to be our escorts; were we to expect Roman Catholic and Free Church chaplains to join Invincible, if so when are they likely to be with us? But I could get no definite answers at that time.

The new commander, Bruce Trentham, joined. He was a very different character from John Rimington, but he seemed very dynamic, experienced and a very nice man. I looked forward to working with him.

My preparations for 'Orient 92' included calling on the Admiral who would command the task group, Jonathan Brigstocke, to 'make my number' and hopefully pave the way for a good working relationship with him and his staff.

We were alongside for only a few days before sailing again for a 'shake down', once again emphasising the constant need for aircraft and ship to work together, bringing both to a level of efficiency and readiness that could be lost when there's a change of personnel or when a ship has not been to sea for a while.

Aircraft can't fly off the deck if the ship is in harbour so the only place to do that is out in the open sea and the best place, as far as we were concerned, was the Morey Firth once again.

On this occasion, as we sailed, we were joined by HRH the Prince of Wales who embarked to watch the Sea Harriers land on. After we had cleared Portsmouth, he would fly off to Kent when we had rounded the 'corner'. He was to be joined by the young Princes William and Harry. This, of course, caused a ripple of excitement when it was first revealed. It seemed that Prince Charles had been taught to fly by our Commander Air, Warren Benbow, and they had remained in touch, so when an invitation for a short passage in the ship was extended, the invitation was accepted.

Preparations were made to entertain the young princes. On the day, one of the seamen's mess decks had been transformed into a pirate's lair. The mess members were dressed as pirates and suitable outfits had been made for the boys. All was ready for a most memorable day at sea. In the event, Prince Charles arrived but without his sons. We had to sail on time and the Prince, having toured the ship and met many of the ship's company, joined the HODs for tea on the Admiral's Bridge before flying off into Kent.

He was very interested in each of us and our responsibilities but later that evening I spoke to Warren who said that Price Charles had been deeply embarrassed by the absence of the Princes and had apologized for their non-appearance given all the preparations.

Heading north we sailed up the east coast of England until we reached the east coast of Scotland and the Moray Firth. The weather has deteriorated badly so flying was prevented but the church services the following day were unaffected. It seemed strange to be on my own conducting the Morning Service because Richard Madders had left the ship.

Exercise 'Teamwork' commenced on 6 March and we moved into the Norwegian Sea. Over the next couple of weeks we would conduct evolutions with the Navies of other NATO countries in this case, Norwegians, Americans and Canadians. These were conducted on a regular basis which is why the Standing Naval Force Atlantic is such an important facet of NATO's arm. By constant exercising we can understand one another's ships and objectives and so maintain a greater effectiveness to meet any threat at sea.

The following day was a Sunday, 1 March, Saint David's Day. Captain John read the lesson and we had a goodly number at the 1000 morning service and, in fact, at all the services that day. Once again there was a strong Welsh connection in the congregation and on completion of the service the Captain invited us to his cabin for Celtic coffee.

The conditions did not improve over the next few days so there was no flying. The upper decks were out of bounds including the Quarter deck, as the ship was rolling very badly.

Most could not remember her moving about so much in the water. Waves were banging against the side just below my cabin and moving around had to be done with care. That evening at the Command Brief I wedged myself into a corner of the bridge as the waves were breaking over the bows and heavy spray was slamming against the bridge windows. It was quite scary at times. Returning to my cabin, descending the ladders and moving along the passageways, I was reminded of part of Psalm 107; 'They that go down to the sea in ships and occupy their business in great waters. These men see the works of the Lord and His wonders in the deep. For at His word the stormy wind ariseth and lifteth up the waves thereof, and they reel to and fro like drunken men.' How true!

The bad weather continued for a few days, everyone was tired as it was difficult to sleep due to the noise of the wind and sea and the motion of the ship. When the weather eased due to lost time, many flying serials had to take place throughout the day and into the night. Not only our pilots but the USS *America's* pilots too had to catch up on the delays. On 21 March 'Teamwork' came to an end and we moved into the fjords to transfer the Admiral and his staff for their return to the UK.

In appreciation of all the effort made, the Admiral

ordered 'Up Sprits' and at 1100 the tots were issued in the messes. It was one of the few times that I can remember 'Up Spirits' being 'piped' in any of the ships that I had served in.

The following day was the Third Sunday in Lent and the Captain's last Sunday on board the ship, possibly his last Sunday at sea, so he asked to read the lesson. Chief Cook Latham presented him with a 'Bible' cake, which was a work of art. It seemed a shame to cut it but the Captain did and everybody had a slice to wish him well. I hope that it was a memorable time for him.

We arrived off of Portsmouth at 0200 and there was a busy forenoon preparing to go into harbour.

Leave ended on Monday, 20 April and the 22nd there was a handover between Captain John and his relief Captain Fabian Malbon. Captain John departed the ship at 1400. I was sorry to see him go as it had been our third time together. I liked him greatly because he was a gentleman and a brilliant commanding officer and we had shared many experiences.

I had also been contacted by the Mission to Seamen, as it was called then, with a view to transporting Bibles to their mission in Mombasa. I mentioned it to the Captain and he agreed, so a lot of Bibles were delivered to the ship in the week leading up to our sailing. They were stored in the vestry down on 7T and secured for sea. Being away for a long time meant that I had to identify memorial dates so that if we passed over a war grave then we would be able to lay wreaths in memory of those lost. Also, MacMillan Nurses were holding a 'Walk a Mile' event to raise funds and I thought it would be a good idea to join in, even though we would be at sea. I asked the Captain and he agreed so I contacted the organisers and they were delighted not only with support but with the photo opportunity it offered to them and to the ship. So another load of items like balloons and sponsorship forms and posters were delivered and stowed in the vestry. Then I had to ensure that the vestry (when I could get into it) was well stocked with 'church' supplies.

'Orient Express 92' would consist of HM ships, *Invincible*, *Newcastle*, *Boxer* and *Norfolk* and together with RFAs *Olwen* and *Fort Grange* would constitute a task group which would go as far as Japan and then return. We would be calling on the way to a number of ports with a three-week maintenance period in Hong Kong. This would be a great opportunity for families to come and join us. As you can imagine, this caused great excitement within my family. Names of the families who are going to make the trip were gathered and so that they could be kept informed of any changes in the ship's programme.

The next thing was to book accommodation for my family. I obtained a family flat in the Hong Kong Mariner's Club. One Saturday, I received a phone call at home from the manager of the Club asking if I would bring out his collection of records. In return he would help me with accommodation. I readily agreed.

Chapter Twenty-one

Orient Express '92 or The Road to Hong Kong and Other Places'

We sailed for 'Orient Express '92' at 0915 on Tuesday 12 May in Procedure Alpha, having embarked the Band of the Royal Marines who would be with us for the duration. A great treat. It was a very windy and cold May morning. Families were on the Round Tower and it was the last time that I would exit Portsmouth that way. We were all sad to leave our families behind but it was tempered with the excitement of a long deployment and all that that brings.

I had bought a computer some months before and had it with me on my desk. I'd always fought against these things but technology was encroaching. I was able to log details of the visits we made to update families via the 'Cascade' system. This system was intended to inform families of things going wrong but it could also be used to inform families when things went right. So whenever we left a port I recorded what had taken place, then sent it to the main contact back in the UK and from there onward and outward to the families. It was a very quick and effective way to keep families in touch with the ship's progress.

We arrived off Gibraltar where we just touched in order to land the members of the press who had sailed from Portsmouth with us. The weather was misty for the next few days and it was quite eerie running on the flight deck when the upper works were shrouded in mist. Please don't think that this was just an extended cruise and that we were on a 'jolly', the reason we were going was because all goodwill visits extend Britain's influence in different parts of the world, particularly the Far East. But it was also an opportunity to exercise with different navies as we went along.

Exercise 'Dragon Hammer' was the first of many and involved ships and aircraft of a number of nations and was very much a continuous training process. On the 10 May we transited the Straights of Messina and 'Dragon Hammer' ended that afternoon.

We arrived at Piraeus, the main port of Athens, and held the cocktail party that evening. There was another chaplain on the deployment, Charles Howard, a lovely man whom I've known for some time. He was looking after the escorts. Charles paid me the compliment of calling on me that evening and we retired to my cabin to chat and consume a libation or two.

On Tuesday, 26 May we sailed from Piraeus. The weather was awful, with heavy rain. There weren't many people on the jetty to watch us leave in Procedure Bravo. Just to ensure that you are convinced that this was not just a 'jolly' we went to action stations at 1300 and remained in this state throughout the rest of the afternoon.

Later that afternoon another incident occurred when a 'Harrier' ditched right alongside the ship. The pilot, Peter Wilson, an RAF pilot who had seen the error of his ways and was transferring to the RN, had been approaching to land on when the aircraft lost all power and dropped on the edge of the deck before slowly toppling over the side. As it went over he ejected at an angle of 45°. Fortunately, he was not hurt and the sea boat was launched to pick him up without any difficulty

On our way along the Mediterranean we crossed over areas where ships had been sunk in wartime, one of which was *HMS Kipling*. We held a memorial service for *Kipling* on the Quarterdeck in the afternoon and one of the wreaths was laid on the water.

When we entered Port Suez, at the top of the Canal, the ship was stopped for a while awaiting a Canal pilot to take us through. Whilst we were stopped, a number of people joined the ship including Richard Madders, the Roman Catholic chaplain, who was back with us until Hong Kong. During this lull, we were instantly entertained by the 'hully gully' men. They were magicians who showed tricks with live chickens and as they were doing so called out 'Hully gully' and then you pay them a few 'ickies' (foreign coins). Then there were the vendors who were selling 'Rolex' watches for a 'fiver', they were all imitations of course but quite a lot of our people bought them as gifts to take home. It was all good fun and I was very confident that those young people who are on board, many of whom had not been in the Navy that long, were having an experience which they would never otherwise have had.

As one of the Wrens said to me, 'When I think of my sister at home, or my friends, I'm so glad I'm here because otherwise all I'd be doing is working in a shop.' I couldn't fault the logic in that.

The ship entered the Suez Canal on 4 June. The canal is an amazing work of engineering and unless you transit it you cannot get the full effect.

I got up early the next morning to run around the flight deck and it was just an extraordinary sight. On either side was desert as far as the eye could see. It was hot, so hot in fact that later that day one of the cooks fried an egg on the deck!

Emerging from the Canal into the Indian Ocean we were greeted by a school of dolphins playing around the bows of the ship. No matter which ocean, it is a wondrous sight.

That evening there was a flight deck barbecue and horse racing which did not descend into the chaos that the previous one had. It was a delightful evening and as it had been extremely hot during the day, it was still warm and I enjoyed sitting on the 'round down' (stern) of the flight deck, watching the sun go down. It was very calming.

Sometimes late in the evening I would stand at the Quarterdeck rail and gaze at the wake. In tropical waters, the propellers turning would cause plankton to rise to the surface which created a phosphorescence in the water stretching far behind us. It was quite hypnotic and also very calming.

The following day was the Feast of Pentecost or Whit Sunday. We had a quite a lot of people at the 1000 morning service and what was most pleasing was the number of Junior Ratings there. Mess deck visiting does work. The numbers at the Communion services were pretty constant but there's always room for improvement. 80 people in church, is about 10% of the ships company. How many churches in this country get 10% of the parish in church? I hoped that we were moving in the right direction. Of course it could change from Sunday to Sunday.

In the Royal Navy joining a ship was always done via the quarter deck and it was customary to salute. Now, joining a ship today is not necessarily via the quarterdeck but the custom is to throw up a salute. For hundreds of years the salute was to a Crucifix that was displayed on the quarterdeck and even in the present day, those joining or leaving a ship do not return the salute of the duty watch. They are paying respect to the Crucifix, even though there isn't one there.

In American ships, when joining, a salute is given to the flag on the stern, or fantail as they put it, and then to the duty watch, but not in ships of the Royal Navy. I think the last ship to display a Crucifix was in 1913. However, since the quarterdeck was being used for regular worship on Sundays I approached the Captain and asked if I could re-instate the tradition and have a Crucifix on the quarterdeck. Having established where it would go, he agreed.

I approached 'Chippy' and he made a plain wooden Cross which was affixed to the bulkhead. It was always behind me or whoever was officiating. So every time we had a service on the Quarterdeck the congregation would be facing the Cross. I was very pleased that we were able to reinstate a tradition of practice that had been lying dormant for such a long time. Each Sunday we now had a visible symbol of the Love of God and it saved me having to carry a heavy cross up seven decks.

The CO of 801 squadron which flew the Harriers came to see me and told me that he was very worried about one of his pilots. When I asked why, I was told that, apparently, that afternoon after a 'sortie' the pilot got out of his aircraft, walked down the flight deck, took off his helmet, put it in the middle of the 'round down', walked up and down a couple of times and then booted the helmet over the side.

So I said, 'Yes, of course, I'll see him just so long as he is happy to come and talk to me.' He came to see me and sat behind closed doors and we talked. I quickly gathered that he was very 'down' due to problems at home that were weighing heavily on his mind. 'I've blown it, haven't I?' he said. 'In what way?' I asked. 'Well, kicking my helmet over the sided, they'll throw the book at me.' 'Oh, I don't know. Do you want to stay in the Navy?' 'Yes,' he said, 'I love my job.' 'Well, let's see what can be done. Trained pilots are not cast away lightly. But the first thing is to get you home'. Once again on the principle that if someone can be spared then we should allow them home, I went to see his CO and outlined his need. He agreed to the self-paid leave. He was released and left as soon as a flight could be arranged for him.

He returned to the ship in due course. A few days later whilst working with the flight deck crew, they took the risk and asked me to launch an aircraft which I did (no mishaps this time!) and it was this pilot that I launched. He gave me a salute as the aircraft began rolling, which I thought was rather nice and I thanked him later.

The weather had deteriorated and I remarked that it was a bit like the North Atlantic only warmer. The sky was grey with strong winds and the sea state had risen, I gathered that it was called the 'Somali Jet'. The ship was rolling heavily and it was likely to be a bumpy night. The following day the sky cleared and it was sunny and hot. Although the sea remained rough, the winds were easing. On Sunday we 'Crossed the Line' that is The Equator. It was Trinity Sunday and there were over 160 on the quarter deck for the 1000 morning service and both Communion services were well attended. One of the reasons for the large number of people was that the service, in part, commemorated the 10th anniversary of the Falklands War. Richard took the service and I preached. A busy day ensued because at 1100, as soon as the service finished, we had the 'Macmillan Walk a Mile' for the Macmillan Nurses cancer charity. Over 400 of the ships company 'turned to' and completed the walk, raising just under £1000. We 'Crossed the Line' and I escaped being dumped in the pool. But Peter Wilson, whose aircraft had lost power a week or so before, was accused by 'King Neptune' of dumping scrap in the ocean and he was duly punished. It was great fun.

When were arrived in Mombasa a number of officers were leaving us, so after they were dined out an RPC (Request the Pleasure of your Company) took place on the Quarterdeck with a 'Safari' theme. We had the pleasure of the Royal Marine band playing for us.

We arrived at Mombasa on 16 June. Within an hour of arriving, the Mission to Seamen chaplain arrived to collect the Bibles that we had stored for him. So I managed to muster a small working party and we got the Bibles up from 7T, down the gangway and into his minibus.

I also had to make sure that the working party to attend the *Brilliant* memorial was still available. A few years before, *HMS Brilliant* was off the coast of Kenya and sent the helicopter into Mombasa to collect mail. During the flight the door on the helicopter came adrift and flew into the rotors and the helicopter crashed with the loss of six lives.

A memorial had been erected in their memory on the beach not far from Mombasa. When any RN ships put into Mombasa they send a working party to do any heavy maintenance work on the memorial. I had put out an appeal on Daily Orders and had a number of volunteers who wanted to help at the crash site.

That evening at the cocktail party I met a couple, Daphne and Arnold, who tended the memorial, kept it clean and put flowers there from time to time. They asked if they could come with us and I readily agreed, as they knew exactly where it was.

Next morning we left the ship at 0800 and collected Daphne and Arnold, arrived at the memorial around 0900 and worked until we could do no more. It was very hot and very tiring work but we did all that we could to maintain the memorial to these young men who died in tragic circumstances.

The following day Daphne and Arnold arrived and took a few of us on a sightseeing tour of Mombasa. We dropped in to the Mombasa Club for coffee and they introduced us to a number of people. We would be returning to the club that evening for a mess dinner, which turned out to be a fabulous occasion when over 100 officers sat down to dine on one long table on the main terrace.

We were all dressed formally in tropical mess undress, which is white mess jackets and black ties, it was the smartest rig that we had. It was a splendid evening, very warm but not overly so and the most enormous moon was shining that night. So the toast was 'La bella luna', as well as the traditional and Loyal toasts.

Unfortunately one or two people had been imbibing for quite some time before dinner and the First Lieutenant fell face forward into his soup. The Captain sitting opposite said, 'Please, will somebody retrieve that officer. It will be an ignominious end to his career were he allowed to be drowned in a bowl of soup.' So 'The Jimmy' was hoisted from the bowl and quietly escorted from the table so that he could sober up, which he did, and re-joined us in time for the pudding. I said the Grace in Swahili. That afternoon when Daphne and Arnold brought us back to the club, I cornered one of the stewards who spoke the local dialect and asked him to translate a Grace for me? I hope that what I said was the Grace I'd written and not something else! I still have the Grace, so if there are any Swahili speakers who read this book then I'd be glad of your advice. But it was a lovely evening and one which will live long in my memory.

On the Sunday there was a service at the Mission to Seamen to which we were invited but because so many people were away from the ship there wasn't a great turnout. Nevertheless, we were, once again, made very welcome. That evening Charles Howard joined Daphne, Arnold and myself for dinner at which we thanked them profusely for all their kindness. We sailed next morning after what had been a very successful visit which everyone enjoyed. I was interested to see what contributions we would get towards the deployment video.

On 27 June we had a band concert which was superb. The Royal Marine band is always outstanding and this was no exception. On completion of the concert we had supper with the Captain. The following day was Sunday with the usual church services. Sometime before, Dento and I thought it was about time that we use the flight deck a bit more so we had planned an upper deck movie night. The Chief Boatswain's Mate (the Buffer) arranged some very large sheets of white canvas which were hung from the side of the 'island' facing the flight deck and the projector would be played onto that. That afternoon I joined the HODs team for a 'brighter' cricket competition played on the flight deck. Let me explain, the balls were made of layers of rolled up 'duck tape' and hitting them was not easy, though some did go over the side. Other than that, the rules were the same. In the evening I joined a lot of the ships company to watch the flight deck movie.

The film was pleasant enough but it was the occasion that proved to be superb: being able to watch a film on a gently moving ship under the stars. With most of the lights on the flight deck turned off it was pretty dark and the vast panoply of the heavens was arrayed above us. It was magnificent. Yet again I wondered at the imagination of God. It really was quite an occasion.

'Paradise Island' aka Diego Garcia

Next day 29 June at 1430 we arrived at Diego Garcia, which is a horseshoe-shaped atoll with an American naval base, although the atoll is actually 'British'. When President Roosevelt gave us 50 clapped out destroyers early in the Second World War, he received in exchange bases around the globe, one of which was Diego Garcia. We received a great welcome there and we were also able, at very short notice, to arrange a football match between ourselves and *HMS Norfolk*. It was a good game and we won 3 - 2.

That night we invited the Americans to a Mess Dinner which they enjoyed very much.

The following morning, Dento and I went along the beach inside the horseshoe-shaped lagoon. We heard a slapping sound and when we looked there was a fish's tail coming out of the water and slapping the surface, if I hadn't seen it I would not have believed it but it is true and I have never seen anything like it since. As we walked along there were large land crabs scuttling about but it didn't deter us, as I was determined to swim in the Indian Ocean. This I was able to do but we were warned not to swim at night because sharks came inside the reef.

We went to the 'O' Club for lunch and I wish we could have stayed longer, it was so beautiful. That evening we dined with the Commander and others who provided supper They had caught barracuda off the reef that morning which was cooked in the Wardroom galley. I have to say it was a really nice fish. We sailed the following morning.

On 9 July at 0830 we arrived in Singapore in Procedure Alpha. The following day was a Sunday, and we were invited to go to a service at the Mission to Seamen despite the torrential rain. Later that afternoon the rain stopped and we watched *Invincible*'s football team beat the Singapore Guards 4-3. It was a really good game and the Guards were an excellent side, so our training had borne fruit. We sailed from Singapore the following morning.

Nothing much happened over the next few days apart from the usual shipboard routines and the Thursday night quiz. Sunday dawned and the clocks went forward. We were now eight hours ahead of the UK. We arrived in Japan in Procedure Alpha on Thursday 23 July.

Japan

We were to berth in the Japanese Naval base of Yokosuka. There was a long approach, with ships on either side of the approach. All were lined with sailors of the Japanese Navy shouting a greeting in unison. It was well orchestrated and sounded like 'Banzai', it couldn't have been but it sounded like it. I found it very disconcerting. Not long after the gangway was opened, I was visited by four chaplains of the United States Navy who came to welcome us, which was kind of them. One of them, Mike Mueller, returned to drive us around and show us the chaplaincy, which was very grand in comparison to the facilities that we had in Portsmouth. Their chaplaincy was not just a chapel and offices but it incorporated a library, an extensive kitchen and conference facilities. It really was very impressive but then that's the difference in budgets.

He also took us around the Naval Base, which was

quite interesting because bit by bit the Japanese were taking back the base from the Americans. The Japanese Navy was twice the size of the Royal Navy and it showed. We went back on board having had a very extensive tour of the dockyard in time to change for the cocktail party.

The following day was Defence Industries Day when the ship was used as an advertising platform for defence sales. The HODs were expected to act as hosts on the Quarterdeck and there were displays of weapons systems from a variety of British companies. We were told by one of the 'reps' that the Japanese did not like the 'hard sell' but preferred a 'patient approach'. This made such an event on board *Invincible* ideal, as continuity was appealing to them. *Invincible* was built by Vickers at Newcastle. The most historic battle cruiser of the Japanese Navy was the *Mikasa,* built by Vickers at Newcastle in 1902. That sort of continuity was something that impressed them, or so he said.

On Saturday it was very hot and humid. We went to visit the ancient capital of Japan, Kamakura, with its shrines of Hase. From there we went to see the Great Buddha and then on to Tsurugaoka and Hashiman-gu. In the evening there was a fireworks display at the 'O' Club. On Sunday after limited church services I went to do some sightseeing. First, to the battle cruiser *Mikasa*. Commissioned in 1902, the *Mikasa* is a veteran of the Battle of Tsushima when Admiral Togo destroyed the Russian fleet. Serving on board at the time was a young sub-Lieutenant Yamamoto who led the attack on Pearl

Harbour in 1941. The *Mikasa* now resided outside the gates of the Naval Base set in concrete.

We toured the ship and, to our amazement, below decks, at the stern, was a shrine to Lord Nelson and Lady Hamilton. We carried on to see central Tokyo but I wasn't really impressed. To be fair, we didn't have a great deal of time, some went on the 'bullet train' to Mount Fuji but that was an overnight stay and I couldn't go, so we just went to Tokyo. Our time in Japan was short so we couldn't really do it justice. We sailed on Monday 27 July.

Pusan

A few days later we arrived at Pusan, Korea. On the first evening we went to a restaurant called, The John Wayne (I am not kidding!). An interesting experience and the food wasn't that bad.

The cocktail party took place on the evening afterwards but curiously very few of the guests appeared. It was one of the least populated cocktail parties that I've ever been to. On Saturday 1 August there was what was called a 'culture' trip, when we went by coach to visit various shrines and things within the life and history of Korea.

I have to say, Korea is a country that's been fought over so long and so often and surrounded by such powerful neighbours that it doesn't really have much of a personality. Lovely people but a bleak landscape in many ways, always in a state of readiness for war.

As we travelled in the coach, alongside the road were 'blast' walls, small walls erected to deflect the effect of jet engines, so that, in the event of a war, the roads could be used as runways. The nation was prepared for conflict whenever it may come. We visited a number of temples including a 'snake' temple, which I refused to enter because I can't stand snakes. Overall, it was an interesting trip and we got back to the ship in the late afternoon.

The next day was Sunday and I had an early morning service but again because so many people were away there was no 1000 service. We did have a party in the afternoon for children from a nearby orphanage which was a great success.

A few days later came another Defence Industries Day so the HODs again acted as hosts and provided coffee and then a buffet lunch on the Quarterdeck. In the afternoon the football team played the Republic of Korea Naval side on a sand pitch in sweltering heat. At half time the score was 1–1, unfortunately the effects of heat and their fitness told and we lost 6-1. The boys gave a good account of themselves but they were outclassed. At 0900 on Wednesday, 5 August we sailed from Pusan in Procedure Alpha.

Hong Kong – the shopping paradise

On 13 August late in the forenoon, we entered Hong Kong harbour in Procedure Alpha with a gun salute to the Governor of the Colony (as he represented the Queen).

Once alongside, Doc and I went to *HMS Tamar*, the shore establishment in which the dockyard sat, to make courtesy calls. Then on to the Mariner's Club to ensure that all the arrangements were in place for the families' stay. There was also a change in clerical personnel. Richard Madders left us to be replaced by John Jochin, a Church of Scotland and Free Church chaplain who was due to be with the group for the remainder of the deployment.

Next day was hectic. The Mission to Seaman chaplain called early to collect the Bibles which had to be brought up from the vestry on 7T and he kindly took them and me to the Club and thence to the airport in time for the families arrival at 1130.

The following day we had the cocktail party but for the next two weeks it would be part ship and part shopping and part tourism for me. I will relate only the more interesting events.

Hong Kong is probably the most vibrant city that I've ever been to, though I dare say that, sadly, it has now changed because the Chinese government has changed the rules but at the time it was vibrant and alive and so exciting. As far as the shopping was concerned, the desire on the part of my family ranged from clothes to cameras, to clothes, to furniture and back to clothes. So visits to Stanley Market, the Night Market, Prince Edward Market, the Jade Market and the street markets, as well as the main stores, were all visited ad nauseum over the next two weeks.

Visits included the space museum and planetarium; Ocean Park, where we were as wet as the dolphins because it hammered down with rain the whole time; Lantau Island and a visit to mainland China by boat up the Pearl River. A highlight for my wife was an invitation, along with all the other wives, to tea at Government House, which she enjoyed enormously.

There were also a number of concerts given by our band of Royal Marines, one of which took place in a bar called 'Ned Kelly's'. The resident band had been given the night off but they turned up to listen as well. The place was packed with sailors and marines and it really was a memorable musical extravaganza. In other words, a thumping good evening.

Lots of sporting fixtures took place while we were in Hong Kong but I only attended the football. They had a number of games, one of which was against a local, allegedly first division side but the lads were doing well and we beat them, which was splendid since keeping fit at sea is not easy.

All too soon the time came for the families to return home and on Friday, 28 August they departed at 2030. It had been a hectic two weeks, which I hoped they enjoyed, and prayed for safe journeys for them all.

Shortly after the families had gone home, Dento, the Doc and I were in the bar of the Mariner's Club having a drink and Dento was helping himself to peanuts from a bowl on the table. He thought that they were free but they weren't. An irate Chinese gentleman said 'Oi. Those are mine.' Profuse apologies were offered and we fell into conversation. I asked him if he could recommend a restaurant and he gave me his business card (great ones for business cards are the Chinese) and said, 'Take this, go to' and he named a street 'and give to my cousin. He owns the restaurant which is called,' and he gave us the name. So we went and when we got there a very large Chinese 'bouncer' was turning people away. My two companions said 'Right, who's going to ask?' They decided that the vicar should take the flak. So, mustering my courage, I offered the bouncer the card. He simply grunted and went inside. He came back a few moments later and grunted 'OK' and in we went.

It was fantastic. We were the only Europeans there and it was filled with Chinese families of all ages. We were made so welcome and it was wonderful to see whole families dining together. It was a good day; we had kept busy since there was a major anti-climax with the families having gone back. The ideal thing would've been to sail almost immediately but of course we couldn't.

Our time in Honk Kong had been so enjoyable and the people were smashing. I would have liked to return and work there in a parish when I left the Navy but it wasn't to be.

We sailed from Hong Kong in Procedure Alpha in the afternoon of Wednesday 2 September at 1840.

Being back at sea, it was a case of generally settling

back into the usual routines. *HMS Newcastle* had sailed at 1115, they were on the way to the Philippines to help with typhoon relief. John Jochin sailed with them.

It was surprising how quickly we settled back into ship- board routines. On Saturday night we dined out a number of people who were due to leave at our next port of call. Sunday services took place as usual. It was good to get back to sea even if it was only for a few days, because next morning at 1000 we arrived at Singapore in Procedure Alpha.

Singapore and Gin Slings!

Upon arrival in Singapore the ship went to the Naval Base at Sembawang. This used to be a Royal Navy base but, since the East of Suez policy, there had been a gradual withdrawal with the Americans now running the base. We were working tropical routine for the entire visit which meant that most mornings we would be on board doing whatever needed to be done, with work finishing at midday.

That evening we renewed our friendship with the cricket club and were made very welcome. *HMNZS Waikato,* a Leander class frigate, had arrived and was moored ahead of us, it was good to see a Leander frigate again, I had many happy memories of serving in them.

On Friday I went shopping and bought a number of elephants (china ones) and I wasn't the only one. There was a parade of elephants up the gangway and a lot of them found their way to the vestry. Having bought them the problem we had was getting them back to the ship? Opposite the compound was a shopping mall and outside the mall was a mini bus and a couple of New Zealand sailors sitting in it. We asked if they could kindly take us back to the ship, since their ship was parked just ahead of us and they were happy to oblige. When they dropped us off they asked if there was any possibility that our engineering department had a particular 'spanner?' Leanders are steam ships, whereas *Invincible* was a gas turbine, so whether we had what they wanted was something I did not know so I said I would ask the engineers. The lack of this item was the reason they had broken down and limped into harbour and getting such a 'spanner' sent from New Zealand would take some time. So I went to see the MEO and asked if he had this 'item' and he said 'Tell them to ask their MEO to call to see me for a coffee and we'll see what we can do'. I passed the message on and I gathered that we were able to help. They eventually fixed the problem and sailed for home. New Zealand had cut back its defence expenditure drastically but when a ship is unable to sail because of the lack of a spanner then doesn't that bear out the nursery rhyme 'for want of a nail a battle was lost?' So those New Zealand sailors can thank the 'elephants' for getting them home!

A number of events took place on the Saturday which are worth noting, first our rugby team were thrashed by the New Zealanders 37-10 (nothing changes!) and the

Royal Marine Band 'Beat Retreat' on Singapore Cricket ground much to the delight of the local inhabitants. This was one reason why the band was on board, to promote Great Britain wherever we went. In the numerous cocktail parties that were held in each port, the evening always came to a spectacular end with the band coming onto the flight deck via the aircraft hoists. Guests would be gently ushered to the sides and the band would suddenly rise up from the depths of the ship and a musical marching display would commence concluding with ceremonial 'Sunset' when the White Ensign was lowered. It never failed to impress me let alone the guests!

After a visit from the local US Navy chaplain and discussing with him our roles in our respective Navies, Dento and I visited 'Raffles' the world famous hotel and supped 'Singapore Slings'. When in Singapore! I do not remember much about the drink itself but it was very expensive. We came away with the glasses as souvenirs. I still have mine.

The following morning on the Wednesday I had been asked to organize a memorial service at Changi jail. In 1945 members of 819, 1833 and 1839 squadrons had been shot down during the raid on the oil refineries at Palembang. They were captured and imprisoned in Changi. In August 1945 after the Japanese had surrendered, they were taken to a nearby beach and beheaded. The members of the current 819 squadron asked if I would be prepared to do a memorial service for them in the little chapel at Changi. I devised the service and obtained permission of the prison chaplain. It was only a short service, with a short homily followed by the laying of the wreath by the Squadron Commander in memory of those brave sailors. It was very moving.

Back to sea

We sailed from Singapore on Thursday 17 September in Procedure Bravo as there was no crowd to see us off and it was raining. When it rains in Singapore, it rains!

During the course of the day I had been asked by a member of the Admiral's staff to say prayers for his late father-in-law who had been killed whilst flying a 'Sea Vixen' fighter. The 'Sea Vixen' was an aircraft of the Royal Navy of the 1960/70s and it had a dreadful record. Over 50% of them crashed. There was a high proportion of pilots killed and he happened to be one of them. There were just three of us on the Quarterdeck, I said prayers and a wreath was laid on the water.

The usual church services took place the following day. It felt strange including my brother's name on the list of sick relatives for I had received news that he was gravely ill. The following Friday 25 September just after mid-day we held another memorial service, this time for *HM Ships Prince of Wales* and *Repulse* which were lost to Japanese air action on 10 December 1941. They sailed from Singapore without air cover to attack the landings further along the Malayan coast. They were in the South

China Sea when they were attacked by a large force of Japanese aircraft and went down with great loss of life.

Our divers had gone down to renew the White Ensigns which continue to 'fly' from both ships. It had become the practice that any RN ships that passed this way renewed the Ensigns. So, as we approached the war graves, the ship's engines were stopped and the service was held from the flight deck with the Admiral laying the wreaths on the water. Over the next couple of days a number of exercises were held including a full NBCD exercise where we all had to get into the protective suits and respirators. Training continued apace no matter where we were or what the weather was like.

On Friday 2 October, late in the afternoon, we came to anchor off the island of Pulau Tioman which enabled the ship's company to go ashore and have a banyan. We raised anchor late on Saturday night. After setting sail and having secured for sea, the Wardroom dined the doctor out, as he was leaving the ship to fly home to a new appointment. It was to be the last 'Sundowner's' on board and I was sorry to see him go. Sunday services were as usual and on Monday 5 October we arrived at Penang.

As I've said previously, 'Deltex' signals are always difficult and I heard the 'pipe' and nothing more. So it meant that it was not for me, but I was summoned by the Commander who told me that the signal was for the Deputy Marine Engineering Officer (DMEO), stating that his brother had died.

He said, 'He knows, the Captain has informed him

and we are thinking of giving him dinner tonight and getting a few drinks down him'. I said, 'I wish you'd spoken to me first because I don't think that's a good idea. Alcohol and grief are not necessarily suitable companions.' 'Oh, it'll be all right', he said. So that was that. When I went into the Wardroom that evening there were a group senior officers standing at the bar having coffee having had dinner and drinks. I left and went to the studio but when I came back I was confronted by the Commander who said, 'Oh, there you are. We were having a drink with Peter and he suddenly collapsed in tears and we put him in your cabin. That's OK isn't it?' 'Right,' I said, 'thank you very much. I did warn you, I'd better go and pick up the pieces.'

I went to my cabin and there was the poor chap sitting with his head in his hands. I closed the door and sat down quietly and waited until he looked up. I have never believed in swamping people with lots of words when they are in tears and grieving. Best just to sit silently and let them cry. Eventually, he looked at me and said, 'I'm awfully sorry to blub like this.' 'Don't be daft,' I said, 'you were close to your brother, why should you not cry for him and your loss? I can do a number of things now, I would very much like to pray for you, your brother and your family but if that doesn't sit well with you we can just talk or not. What would you like from me now?' 'A prayer and talk but I warn you I may start crying again.' So I said a prayer for his brother and we sat for a while in silence and then he began to talk about his brother and the times they had as boys.

Eventually, he said, 'I think I'm ready for sleep.' His cabin was directly opposite mine so I said, 'You know where I am if you need to talk during the night or go for a walk and you want company, all you have to do is bang on the door.' Next morning, arrangements were made to fly him off so that he could go home to be with his family. He eventually returned to the ship and came to see me and said, 'I am very grateful to you, thank you very much.'

At the next HODs meeting, although it was not on the agenda, I very emphatically pointed out to them that when it comes down to dealing with matters of grief I had a little bit more experience than they and added, 'When I said that getting somebody pissed is not a good idea then please listen to me, because incalculable damage could be done if you get it wrong'. There was a stunned silence but the point went home.

Penang

We arrived at Penang on the Thursday afternoon. Because there were a lot of people leaving, something like 30% of the ships company would be changing over, there were departmental runs ashore planned. Doc was being taken to shore by the sick bay team and Dento was saying farewell to his assistant. I had no plans so I changed into Red Sea rig and walked into the Wardroom and Wren Steward Thomas asked if I was going ashore and I said, 'No.' 'That's a pity,' she said, and I thought, 'She's right', so I said, 'You are so right. Belay my food order, I'm off!'

I went back to my cabin, changed into 'civvies' and went down the gangway where I was accosted by a lot of rickshaw drivers who wanted my custom. I said, 'No thank you, I'm going to walk up through Georgetown.' 'Oh, Tuan, it is very dangerous, come in my rickshaw.' But I walked, aiming for the Eastern & Orient Hotel. I walked past the old fort constructed in Victorian days and went up to the hotel, which was lovely. I went in through the front door and found a hallway panelled in teak. On the left there was a small bar. I went in and the barman, in a white, high collared jacket asked if I'd like a drink and was I intending to stay for dinner. I said yes to both questions and he summonsed the maitre d'. He came almost at once and offered me the menu. Having finished my drink I was shown to my table and, apart from a small party of elderly Australian, who might have been veterans of the Second World War, the place was empty.

I was just coming to the end of my meal when elderly musicians gathered on the stage and began 'tuning up'. Then at the appropriate time an elderly Malay lady in a powder blue Cheong Sam dress, split to the thigh, stalked across the floor, climbed onto the stage, tapped the microphone and began to sing 'There'll be bluebirds over the white cliffs of Dover.' I felt like a rubber planter down from the hills for a dirty weekend. It was absolutely extraordinary. The Australians in the corner were singing along with gusto. When it was polite to do so, I got up to leave but the maitre d' asked me if I would like a drink.

After affirming his question he said 'You look like a whiskey soda man,' and I agreed and asked him to join me. With great reluctance he did so and he told me that his father had been maître d' there, as had his grandfather when the Japanese had arrived and taken over the hotel as officers' accommodation. He said it was a terrible time but I was delighted in the fact that the hotel hadn't changed since then and I had a lovely evening, albeit on my own.

I have subsequently found out that the Eastern & Orient Hotel has changed radically. The description to me indicates that it has lost all its character and become very modern, so I'm glad I was able to go there before that happened. When I got back to the ship Dento was complaining he hadn't had a very good night and I said, 'Well, you should've come with me.'

The following day on 9 October we sailed from Penang but before we did Phil called to say farewell. I was sorry to see him go but I was sure our paths would cross again. With such a change of personnel, much training had to be done and ship's routines had to be impressed upon the new people. Later that night the clocks went back one hour, a true indication that we were on our way home.

Next day was Sunday with church services at the usual times but the 1000 service was a Harvest Festival and once again we had the Harvest loaf complete with mouse and which, on completion of the service, was distributed around the congregation with lashings of butter!

The following Sunday afternoon we had a village fete on board. It wasn't to raise funds but just a means of entertainment and each mess had to come up with a stall. It was very good fun and we even had clay pigeon shooting off the stern of the ship. It was very warm and sunny and the sea was calm, so a good afternoon was had by all. We were fast approaching Abu Dhabi and on Tuesday morning 24 military VIPs came on board for a tour of the ship and lunch. They were very hard work. That evening the Trafalgar Night dinner was brought forward and went very well, as it always does. I said the Graces and led the singing of 'Rule Britannia' and the Captain made a very good speech.

Abu Dhabi - Gold and sand

On 24 October we arrived in Abu Dhabi and prepared for the cocktail party that evening.

We came alongside at 1130 in Procedure Alpha and as soon as the gangways were cleared, notices went up offering various coach trips, so I booked for a trip to Dubai City. One of the guests at the cocktail party was the chaplain of the St Andrew's Centre. It seems that Abu Dhabi was created by BP from a gigantic sand bar and in return for oil rights they set up the local sheik as ruler. In return he built a church for the oil workers. As soon as the church was completed, he built the biggest mosque outside Mecca right alongside it. Then St Andrews was no longer deemed to be a church but a 'centre'. Subtle opposition to the Christian Faith.

The chaplain told me that he was constantly watched by the Islamic police and if an Arab came into the centre and asked for a Bible and he gave it to them, he and his family would be expelled within a few hours. He had to be very careful of 'agent provocateurs'. If the enquiry was genuine and if caught, that person and his family could be put to death for deserting Islam. The following day the trip commenced at 0800. The coach went along a very straight road with flat desert on both sides. It was quite boring with not a lot to see. We had a tour of Dubai City which included a desert fort, which reminded me of the fort in the book 'Beau Geste'. Having said that, there was not a great deal of interesting things to see. Most wanted to visit the gold markets, the 'souks' and the supermarkets. I bought some fruit and a few souvenirs and went back to the ship.

We met some very kind and interesting people and went to a number of private clubs for lunch and dinners but really Abu Dhabi was just a major shopping opportunity. The Commander bought a car, Dento bought a carpet and I bought a rug. I didn't really want it but the chap kept pestering and in the end I got it for £10.

We sailed 0900 on the Sunday morning. I'd had a number of requests for baptisms from sailors who were getting married on our return. The incumbents of the churches in which they were getting married insisted that they had to be baptised. I don't necessarily agree with that but that's what they had to do. I therefore organized a baptismal course when, during a few sessions we talked about baptism and its meaning so, even though they were being 'dragooned' into it, I felt that they should be prepared and at least understand what it was that they were doing.

It was an opportunity for me to make statements about the Christian Faith to young people from different messes about what they were asking of God. They went back to their messes and without a doubt told others about what we were doing because during my mess deck visits, there were quite a few questions about baptism, about the Christian faith and about how marriage in church is different.

It reminded me once again that chaplaincy in the Armed Services is the cutting edge of evangelism because we were dealing with young people who have rarely been touched by the church. It was a glorious opportunity to make a statement for the Faith. One of the downsides of chaplaincy is that you rarely ever see the results of your endeavours. I don't know whether the Holy Spirit touched the lives of those young people but I sincerely hope so.

The following day was Sunday the 8th before Christmas and it was also All Saints Day. The baptisms I mentioned above took place during the 1030 Morning Service on the Quarterdeck. It was quite a moving service and a lot of people attended, including many from the mess decks of those being baptised. That afternoon there were divisional practices ready for Remembrance Sunday. Preparations for our homecoming took place with advanced leave parties leaving the ship to fly to Brize Norton because when we arrived back, they would have had their leave and so would take over the running of the ship while everybody else had their leave. There was an NBC exercise in the morning and yet again we climbed into protective suits and donned respirators but when the exercise was over, it was very good to walk around the flight deck or Quarterdeck and get a breath of fresh air.

Tuesday 3 November was All Souls Day so the day before was All Hallow's Eve. It is the day when the dead are prayed for. So I placed an announcement in Daily Orders that if anyone wanted a loved one prayed for, to let me know and their names would be offered at the mid-day Requiem Mass. I had just got out of bed when the phone rang and it was Dento who said, 'Are you aware that the deck outside your cabin is littered with letters and cards?' So I opened the door and sure enough there was a lot of 'mail.' Each cabin had a sort of mailbox fixed to the door, into which things like Daily Orders were placed, mine was overflowing with post. So, having made the announcement on Daily Orders and on TV I was inundated with requests for prayers for grannies, mothers, fathers and so on.

Yet again I was surprised at the depths of thought that many sailors had about faith; they may not come to church but they saw value in prayer. I'm not sure if, for some, it might be a bit of superstition, but it showed that by making those announcements people were aware of the chaplain and the values of the Church. We could have an effect on the lives of those we served, whether they come to church or not.

The Holy Land or at least Haifa

We had been due to a visit Mumbai but when we were out in the Far East, the Foreign Office had requested a change to our programme and we were diverted from Mumbai to Haifa in Israel. I have no idea why, nobody told us but ours 'was not to reason' so we arrived in Haifa at 1100 on 6 November in Procedure Alpha. Of course, our people wanted to see the Holy Land so the Captain and I talked about this beforehand, because the Sunday was Remembrance Sunday and we would have to mark it with Ceremonial Divisions, It was decided that the ship's company would be divided into two watches. The first watch would get away to tour Jerusalem and other parts of the Holy Land but they had 36 hours within which to do it. Then when they got back for Remembrance Sunday, the second watch would go.

In the afternoon Dento and I went for a walk around Haifa. It seemed a dusty town with not much of interest. Everything was closed with the onset of the Sabbath but we managed to buy postcards and visit a war cemetery.

On Remembrance Sunday there was an 0800 celebration of Holy Communion in the chapel then at 0900 'Divisions Fall In' was piped before the parade service began on the flight deck at 0930. It was a full parade and they were all in 'best blues'. Considering that the boys and girls had not been able to practice drills for such a long time, they were superb and I was very proud of them. It was a beautiful morning too and the flight deck was filled, not only with our sailors and marines but also with representatives of the Israeli Navy and representatives of other allied navies plus dignitaries from the various embassies in Tel Aviv. However, as soon as the service was over we rushed to pack, have a quick lunch and were off at 1200.

We hired a car and drove to Nazareth. Then on to Tiberius and Capernaum. It was getting dark when we eventually reached our hotel in Jerusalem. On Monday we left the hotel at 0900and went down to the old city to visit the Garden of Gethsemane but it was closed! We saw the Brooke Kidron with a supermarket trolley dumped in it and not a lot of water.

The hill outside Jerusalem where the Crucifixion was supposed to have taken place was so covered in tourists that we left and headed back via Jericho. As we drove along, the Parable of the Good Samaritan leaped out of the pages of the New Testament because I could visualize the scene. The land on either side of the road was like a moonscape and I could well see bandits mugging people on that road. We drove on to the Dead Sea. I have a photograph somewhere of me reading a newspaper floating around in it but I couldn't find it, the one in this book is of me waving! The only problem was that any nicks or small cuts on your body, that you may not otherwise be aware of, are instantly found when you get into the water of the Dead Sea! That evening the Israeli Navy gave a reciprocal cocktail party for us, we did the 'mingling' and chatting but it was a dreary affair. It was obvious that they don't hold these things very often.

We sailed from Haifa on Tuesday 10 November. I had written to the Chaplain of the Fleet to ask if he could tell me how long I was to be in the ship and what my next job was going to be and to my surprise I received a letter informing me that my next appointment was to *HMS Excellent* (Whale Island) immediately upon my return which would mean that I would lose a great deal of leave.

On Friday 20 November we arrived at Gibraltar with a beautiful sunrise. The Top of the Rock Race was scheduled for 1400 in aid of Cancer Research and Children in Need. It was a warm day and I came 209th out of 400 runners. My time was 33 minutes, it was the fastest that I'd achieved and that was my fourth time to run the Rock, despite the fact that I was several years older than the first time around.

We sailed from Gibraltar at 1100. The ship was packed with people. The usual services took place and during the afternoon I had to prepare a speech because I was being dined out that night. I was extremely nervous at the prospect.

On 23 November Customs Officers came on board and I cleared customs for Richard Madders, Phil Runchman and myself. On Thursday the 26th the Carrier

Air Group disembarked and HRH Princess Royal came on board at 1000, in awful weather conditions, to welcome us home and to witness the CAG fly off, form up and conduct a fly past salute to her and to the ship. She was then escorted to the hangar to meet members of the ships company after which she came to the Wardroom for tea before disembarking. Later that evening we arrived off Portsmouth and went to anchor and began to ditch all the 'gash' into barges that came alongside. The waste disposal units had broken down some days before and 1200 people can generate a lot of 'gash.' We came along side in Portsmouth at 1330 the next day and 'Orient Express '92' came to an end. On arrival there was a letter from the Chaplain of the Fleet with a slight change of heart, informing me that I could have two weeks leave in addition to the Christmas leave that was imminent. However, I was expected to break leave and complete a hand over with the outgoing chaplain of HMS *Royal Arthur*, Richard Buckley as *Royal Arthur* was to be incorporated into Whale Island. There was no chaplain at Whale Island but my relief, Wynne Jones (another Welshman), was to join on Sunday 6 December so I had just under a week to get my kit off the ship and prepare for his arrival. The hand over duly took place and on Thursday 10 December I left HMS *Invincible*. I was sorry to go but it had been an amazing period in my life, I had met some lovely people and been to some wonderful places and I was grateful for the experience which would live with me forever.

Chapter Twenty-Two

HMS Excellent aka Whale Island

HMS Excellent is affectionately known throughout the Navy as 'Whaley' short for Whale Island which began life as two mud flats in Portsmouth Harbour. They appeared whenever the tide went out and they were known locally as 'Big' and 'Little' Whale because they looked just like the backs of whales. The Navy used to use Portsmouth Harbour for gunnery practice, to test accuracy of cannons which would fire about a mile up the harbour. Because there was a lot of smoke, they needed to be able to watch the fall of shot and they did so from 'Big and Little Whale'. As the Navy changed, the need for dry docks became apparent so army engineers created Portsmouth Dockyard by digging out the docks using convict labour. The spoil from these large holes in the ground were carried by a special railway line constructed over the water to 'Big and Little Whale'. The earth was dumped in between the two and then gradually bit by bit they got bigger and bigger until they merged into one island. As the original sandbars had been used for gunnery purposes it was natural that the newly created 'island' be used for gunnery too so it became the home of Naval gunnery.

Of course, guns were no longer fired up Portsmouth Harbour but the 'island' became the place where instruction was given and became very important indeed to the life of the Navy. One of the most famous gunners to have qualified at *Excellent* was Petty Officer Edgar Evans who came from my part of the country. He was born in Rhosilli on the Gower Peninsular and educated at the St Helen's Boys School. At the age of 13 he joined the Royal Navy and eventually became part of Scott's ill-fated expedition to the South Pole. The fact that I had become chaplain to *Excellent* was reported in the local newspaper in Swansea and the school, now named Sandfields Junior School asked if I would call and talk to the children about him. This I was very happy to do and presented the school with a badge bearing *Excellent*'s crest and motto.

Whale Island even had a zoo. Ships coming back from overseas deployments of some years duration would often bring back gifts for the sovereign from rulers in other parts of the Empire and these gifts included wild animals. Some went to London Zoo but some stayed at 'Whaley'. Two senior stokers were sent to London Zoo to train as animal keepers. In the 1920s and 30s 'Navy Days' weekends were very popular with the public and Whale Island was the most popular of the shore establishments because it had a zoo including lions and tigers.

When the Second World War was imminent all the big animals were shot and the graves are still there on the north side of the Island. The big animals were never replaced but when I first arrived on Whaley, there were still large aviaries with exotic birds.

However, earlier in this narrative I related that as chaplain to *Nelson* I would go to 'Whaley' to conduct prayers and the ship's company numbered just about 20. The island had been run down as it was no longer required for gunnery and therefore was going to be sold. I understood that interest was shown by such companies as Borg Warner who wanted to build a holiday camp on the Island, or P & O who wanted to turn it into a ferry terminal.

However, I'm reliably informed that a civil servant appeared from the Treasury who informed their Lordships that if the Island was sold the proceeds would go to the Crown because, as it was man made, anything above the waterline belonged to the Crown. So it was decided to economize and rationalise and use the Island as a sort of Naval 'business park' and move several establishments there. So *Royal Arthur, Phoenix,* The Royal Marine Headquarters, the Fire Fighting School would be moved to 'Whaley'. The Regulating School, the Sea Cadet Headquarters, and *King Alfred*, the Royal Naval Reserve unit would remain.

To this busy establishment I had been appointed chaplain and took up my duties on 27 January 1993. My first task was to re-open and refurbish the establishment church dedicated to St Barbara. By way of information, Saint Barbara is the Patron Saint of gunners. The legend has it that she was a Christian girl in Roman times and her father was a wealthy man who wanted to marry her off to another wealthy man neither of whom were Christians. She refused and her father told her that if she did not marry this man he would have her killed. Which apparently was his right under Roman law. She still refused so he had her beheaded and before she died she prayed and offered the Lord her soul. As the blade fell and she died, a thunderbolt came down from heaven and struck the father killing him in turn. As a result, she became the Patron Saint of 'long range snipers'.

The church and chaplaincy had to be re-ordered. The Nave was to remain untouched and the Sanctuary was made a little smaller but the niche that housed a silver image of St Barbara remained. The chaplaincy offices were the other side of the Sanctuary. There were also storage facilities and a meeting room. All of this had to be re-decorated and brought up to acceptable standards including the toilet facilities.

Unlike ships, shore establishments don't go anywhere. Therefore the day by day and week by week routines are more or less the same. I'll try to give you a broad brush look at the establishment and the work that we did and my role within it. The larger units on the island at the time that I joined, were the Regulating [Royal Navy policing] School, the national headquarters of the Sea Cadets and the Royal Naval School of Leadership and Management (RNSLAM) formerly HMS *Royal Arthur*. The regulating school had been there for many years and was the place where those who had successfully applied to become Regulators were trained. The training courses were not large and took place twice a year but we had prayers in the Regulating School once a month, a sort of 'Thought for the Day' with an appropriate prayer attached.

I would also talk to the Regulators about the role of the chaplain and the relationship between Regulators and Chaplains at sea and on land. The whole point was that we, chaplains, were not there to hinder but to help. I always received a very good welcome whenever I went to the school and it always helps to have good working relationships with all. I wish I had known more about the Regulating Branch before I went to sea.

The Sea Cadet headquarters was always welcoming and though I attended the unit to see the cadets from time to time, they needed their own chaplain. I would make a point of calling in to see the staff of the headquarters on my rounds of the 'parish' and if I could do anything for them I would. Occasionally I would go in of an evening to Divisions and talk to the boys and girls and the weekend courses too which came from all over the country. *HMS Bristol,* in which I served, albeit briefly, had been decommissioned but instead of going for scrap she was moored to a special jetty on the Island and became a training base for the cadets. The weekend courses would arrive on Saturday and stay overnight or sometimes for longer, depending on school holidays. They would live on board the ship in mess decks. For them it was a great opportunity to have an experience of what shipboard life was like without actually going to sea. If a course held Divisions on a Sunday morning and requested my presence, I would conduct prayers for them and then spend a short time talking to the boys and girls.

Without doubt the bulk of my time was being involved with, what had been, *Royal Arthur* but since moving to the Island it had become the Royal Naval School of Leadership and Management (RNSLAM). The School ran courses to train Petty Officers and Leading Hands in the skills required at their particular level and the chaplain had an integral part to play. The PO's courses would last one month and the Leading Hands for two weeks. Each course involved instruction including Stress Management, Moral Leadership, Faith and Leadership delivered by me. But my time with them always began with a period titled 'Meet the Bish' when I introduced myself and explained why I was involved in this part of their training. First thing that would happen with the POs course was that they had to select a name for their course, usually an historic figure known to be a great leader like Alexander the Great. I would try and help them to select an appropriate name that they could all agree on. I was able to head them off on a few which would be deemed to be unacceptable or inappropriate, like the Prophet Muhammad!

Instruction from me would be at the same time on the same days each week so I had a great deal of contact with each course. In addition Divisions were held each

Tuesday morning at 0800 and Ceremonial Divisions each Friday morning at the same time. On Friday we sometimes had a special guest to take the salute. I had to deliver prayers and a 'Thought for the Day' each time.

Royal Arthur had been the Navy's Outward Bound Training establishment and that element of training was included in these courses. RNSLAM had taken over the premises used for outward bounding in the Black Mountains above Abergavenny which was a purpose-built centre. From time to time I would join a course going through this phase. It was a great way of getting to know people. Again, this is something all chaplains should do. A far better use of time than many weeks in Dartmouth learning to be the officers they'll never be. Many lively discussions took place within the context of the classroom and whilst 'yomping' over the Welsh hills! The accommodation was spartan but adequate. I could only go if I had cover for the weekday divisions and my instruction periods allowed for it.

At the end of their time the course had to give a short presentation to the staff, the Captain and any senior officers who might be visiting. The presentation took place in the theatre and would be on the life of the person that the course had selected showing the leadership qualities of that person. They were always delivered with a sailor's sense of humour and a tongue in cheek approach. There would always be a course 'run ashore' and invariably I was always invited. There, many former shipmates came through Whaley during my time and it was always good to see them and to know that my time instructing NAMET and GCSE English had not been totally wasted.

From time to time we would also have officers' courses coming through. They included the Divisional Officers Courses when young officers were stepping up to take greater responsibility by becoming Divisional Officers. On one such course, Prince Andrew was a member. The Designated Commanding Officers Course was another to come to RNSLAM, a specially prepared course for those who had been selected to command ships or establishments. At their level it was usually the Chaplain of the Fleet who came and talked to them about the role of the chaplain and the help that the chaplain could be to them at whatever task they were preparing for. Of course, most officers already knew the role of the chaplain but not all came to church and not all were sympathetic to the Church, in fact, some were hostile.

There were those who were Christians, of whatever denomination and whatever rank, who would gravitate to the chaplaincy for a tea or coffee when they had a spare moment. It was always lovely to see them. The times of our instruction periods might vary according to SLAM's programme, I could find myself instructing at odd times including late on a Friday afternoon when most had gone home for the weekend.

Speaking of weekends, there were few church services on Sundays, Unlike St Ann's in the Dockyard, we didn't have a regular congregation. Whale Island had been run down almost to oblivion and a congregation cannot be manufactured if there was no-one there. In fact, I had a visit from the Provost of Portsmouth Cathedral, David Stancliff who came for lunch. His visit was to elicit from me assurances that I wasn't going to try and create a congregation which would reduce the cathedral's congregation. I said if I were to encourage anybody to attend a Naval church it would be St. Anne's not St Barbara's because they would join an already established congregation. I tried on one occasion to organize a service for Mothering Sunday. A great deal of effort went into advertising the service and arranging flowers and refreshments afterwards but the attendance was poor. I suspect that if the Chief's Mess hadn't been holding a special lunch that day then it is likely that no one would have attended.

Most Sundays found me helping out in local parishes to give the clergy some respite. I had a particularly close relationship with St Peter's, Southsea who were without an incumbent at the time. However, I did receive a number of applications for baptism. Now, baptisms can be a thorny subject as far as clergy are concerned. Nearly everyone lives in a parish and ideally, if they want their baby baptised then it is to the parish church they should go. But sailors have this tradition of being able to have their children baptised on board the ship they are serving in and that includes 'stone frigates' or shore establishments. Once an application was made I would arrange to call and see the parents and explain this to them but if, for whatever reason, they still wanted the baptism to take place on board then Plan B came into effect. That was when I insisted that they contact the local priest and let him know that the baptism was to take place because I thought it only fair that he should be informed by the family and perhaps become involved in the life of the family by visiting and encouraging them to attend the parish church. At very least he would know that there was a baptism happening from his 'patch'.

St Barbara's was not licensed for weddings but my Free Church colleagues conducted two in my time with the Registrar present. However, I conducted a number of Blessings of Civil Marriages and it was a great joy to prepare couples for this and meet their families at the receptions which were usually held in the mess to which they belonged. There were also a number of Renewal of Marriage vows. At the other end of the emotional scale, there were quite a few funerals as former members of *Excellent* wanted to be buried from St Barbara's and we were always happy to help the families.

Prayers continued to be conducted in the Lodger Units on a regular basis and sometimes conducted by the RC or CSFC chaplains, but they were not involved in the instruction periods but could occasionally deputise in on divisions. There were a number of notable events in that first year.

On 7 May *HMS Bristol* was re-commissioned in her new role as accommodation centre for the sea cadets and on 26 June the new Sea Cadet Headquarters was dedicated. On 26 July *HMS Phoenix* began the move onto the Island and into their new building. In July Amport week came and in the course of the week I was given information which would have a great effect on me. First, I was told that I would have an assistant but not until next year. His name was John Green, John and his wife had visited *HMS Collingwood* when I was there on an 'aquaint' visit which had taken place about two years before. He had subsequently joined the 'Branch'. It would be great to have someone as capable as John and I looked forward to working with him.

The second item of news was that my Commission was not going to be extended and my next 'job' was likely to be in Portland. I was very disappointed as Portland Naval Base was closing down and the Naval Air Station was earmarked for closure. I would going out with a whimper not a bang. Still, living in Weymouth would be a bonus. 'Ours not to reason why'. 'Whaley' was also home to the Portsmouth Command Field Gun crew who competed against Plymouth Command and the Fleet Air Arm in the Royal Tournament (of blessed memory). To take part they had to be exceptionally fit and training took place throughout the spring and early summer. An exact replica of the 'run' was created and training began after rigorous selection. I used to call in to have a cup of tea with them, they were an exclusive lot but I always had a good welcome.

The year rolled on and 1994 dawned.

On 22 February 1994 I was joined by John Green

who quickly settled in and we were able to share the 'load'.

HMS Phoenix, the Damage Control School had finally arrived on the Island and a new purpose-built unit had been constructed to train courses in damage control. They too were added to the list for visits and prayers and a relationship which had been ongoing for a long time was re-established. Apart from the normal weekly routines, the diary was rapidly filling up with events coming thick and fast.

On 26 April my appointment to Portland was confirmed so I had to think of all the arrangements that would have to be made over the next few months. We had been in our present married quarter for eleven years, and it would be quite a wrench to move. But that's life in a blue suit! On 18 May the Blessing of St Barbara's Church and the Commissioning of *HMS Excellent* took place together. A commemorative plaque was unveiled on the Quarter Deck to mark the occasion.

1994 saw the 50th anniversary of the D-Day landings in Normandy. In 1944 as the Invasion of France neared, Whale Island had become heavily involved in the preparations. The Island was full of armoured vehicles ready for embarkation directly onto heavy landing craft from the slipways on the Island. To commemorate that, a 'Chieftain' tank was driven onto the Island and parked on the parade ground for the duration of the celebrations. The whole Island was geared up to welcome the veterans back as did the rest of Portsmouth. There was even a tent in which counselling could be given. 50 years ago there was no recognition of Post -Traumatic Stress Disorder (PTSD). I had seen a programme on television about the long-term effects of PTSD. This programme outlined a number of personal stories but all showed that at the end of the war people were just demobbed and went back to their lives. Many of them with horrific tales to tell; dreadful experiences which they suppressed. They could keep them suppressed because of their working routines. But once they retired, all the nightmares came back. So we offered a counselling venue for veterans if they chose to take it up. It was nothing more than just listening and talking to them about their experiences if they wished to share them.

On a wider front, on 4 June the Band of the Royal Marines 'Beat Retreat' in Guildhall Square and on Sunday 6 June, there was a Drum Head Service on Southsea Common by the Naval Memorial conducted by the Archbishop of Canterbury. There was a huge congregation and the music was, again, provided by the Band of the Royal Marines. It was broadcast on national television and was a very moving occasion.

HMS King Alfred, the Royal Naval Reserve unit was established on Whale Island and we took part in the Commissioning Service which meant that we had another lodger unit to be involved with.

Later on in the year there was a change of command and we dined Captain out on board *HMS Victory* which was a splendid occasion and a week or so later on 13

October, we welcomed our new commanding Officer, Captain Parker.

1994 rolled into 1995 and there were a few major events which took place. On 16 May the Royal Marine Headquarters building was dedicated and we had a visit from HRH Prince Philip, the Duke of Edinburgh in his capacity as Captain General of the Royal Marines. He made a point of coming over to speak to the clergy who officiated and seemed to get around talking to as many as possible. He was proud of his connections with the Royal Marines.

Earlier in the year during a conversation with the Captain, he asked me how we might begin to unite all the different units so that together, they might begin to see *Excellent* as their home. I suggested that we might begin with a 'Village Fete' and each unit to produce their own stalls. We could open it out to include families. He liked the idea and John and I duly started 'pushing' it It caught on, a date was selected and promulgated and entered in everyone's diaries. It was emphasised that all the proceeds of the day would go to charities both local and national.

John and a friend of his decided to cycle from the Naval Base at Chatham to Whaley. The whole event became titled 'The Great Whaley Village Fete and Family Fun Day'. The Royal Marine printers produced fabulous posters and every unit came up with different stalls. I had put together a small steering committee and everyone set about their tasks with great gusto. The Portsmouth Royal

Marine Band would be playing and there were bouncy castles, roundabouts, swings and all kinds of side shows and food stalls. Even the courses going through joined in with their own stalls.

What we couldn't control was the weather and the forecast was heavy rain. On the morning of the event I telephoned the Naval Air Station at Culdrose in Cornwall and asked what their weather was like and the Met. Officer asked why I wanted to know, so I told him and he said 'What a great day you will have because the rain passed through here an hour ago and it will clear Portsmouth around 1000'.

The Captain sent for me and asked if we should cancel but armed with this knowledge I said, 'No sir, have faith.' 'I hope you're right, 'he replied. A little later as he strolled among the stalls and chatted to the families, he said to me 'I forgot that you have a 'hotline' in these matter' He meant heaven but my hotline was to Cornwall!

John and his friend came cycling onto the parade ground at exactly the right time to announcements on the main tannoy and to much applause. I cannot remember the sum they raised or the overall total that was donated to charity but it was substantial. The aim of the day was achieved, it was the start of the process of blending the units into a whole ship's company and best of all the families had a 'Whale' of a time.

Over the next couple of weeks the routines at Whaley carried on and on 4 August we went on summer leave which was filled with all the things required in moving house including further trips to Weymouth. The new term began on 4 September and with it the 'hand over' to my relief commenced and was to span the next few days. All the Lodger Units had to be visited and introductions made. John Green would fill in the spaces and provide the support to my relief as he had done for me. We said our farewells and I left HMS *Excellent* on Thursday 7 September. I have to say that I too had had a 'Whale' of a time.

Chapter Twenty-three

HMS Osprey – Portland Naval Base

HM Naval Base, Portland had been in existence since 1928. Later, the RN Air Station was added. But since the end of the Cold War, Portland had been seen as surplus to requirements and the run down commenced.

In 1993 Flag Officer Sea Training moved to Plymouth and the Naval Base began to close. It was also decided that the squadrons at the Air Station should be transferred to Yeovilton, so the entire site would shut down. To this closing/closed base I was appointed chaplain. On Saturday, 9 September I drove to Weymouth and the following day I conducted the 1030 Eucharist in Saint Paul's in Portland. The following day I officially took up my appointment and called upon the Captain, Captain Turner. It was an unusual meeting since he was at home suffering from gout but we discussed a number of issues like the Dedication Service for the new St Paul's chapel, my moving house and other issues surrounding the church in *HMS Osprey*. The next couple of weeks would be dominated by my running back and forth to Portsmouth organising the move which involved 'marching out' of one married quarter and 'marching in' to another.

For the first few weeks services continued in the little church just inside the dockyard gates but then once the 'new' chapel was ready we moved there.

It was a very strange situation, the chapel was situated in part of the Wardroom. The Wardroom had been renovated at great public expense and there were plenty of rooms available. So several of these rooms were earmarked for the 'new' chaplaincy and chapel. However, though the church had closed, the chaplaincy, which was outside the dockyard gates, continued to function for several weeks more. With me so far? Anyway, ultimately the entire 'old' chaplaincy closed and the 'new' took over. It was far from an ideal arrangement because anyone who wanted to come to church would have to have a pass to get into the Wardroom so instead of being in neutral and accessible territory, the church was very much seen as being in 'officer country'. But since *Osprey* was closing it was the best option. The old church was quite small and traditional, the new church was a very large room which was carpeted and very plush but it didn't have any church 'ambience' so we would have to try to create one. The congregation was very small but they were a loyal bunch.

Morning and Evening Prayer were said each day and on Sunday there would be a 1030 service of Holy Communion. I had a verger whose name was Janet and local clergy, RC and Free Church came in as 'officiating' chaplains to help as and when required. Each quarter there was a Community Breakfast which was created during the Falklands War and comprised not just Naval personnel but civilian organizations too, with representatives from Social Services and the local authority. It met in the Wardroom at Naval expense and really had outlived its usefulness by the time I arrived and with the closure imminent, it didn't last long.

We were part of the Naval 'deanery' centred in Portsmouth so any meetings meant a long 'flog' for me and for my colleagues at Yeovilton but it enabled me to keep in touch with other chaplains. The squadrons were still working and I spent time moving around from squadron to squadron talking to people. I remember having a very long conversation with HRH Prince Andrew who was senior pilot in 702 Squadron but they too were preparing to move from Portland so it was all a little bit artificial.

Harvest Festival took place on 10 October when the congregation was larger which could have been something to do with the Captain reading the lesson! On 1 November the chapel was Dedicated when some of the Naval church hierarchy came down to officiate.

On 5 December there was a change in command when Captain Turner was relieved by Captain Harvey. Captain Turner had been a great support and was very sympathetic to the situation in which we found ourselves. Captain Harvey would also be a great supporter. He was a delightful man whom I liked instantly and got on with very well. He had been Naval Attaché in the Embassy in Washington and had sailed a yacht across the Atlantic single handed to take up his appointment (his family flew over which was much more sensible!)

On 22 December we went to leave but as usual I held Christmas services. The Midnight Mass saw just half a dozen souls gather and then on Christmas morning there was a service of Holy Communion with carols when were a few more people attended.

1995 merged into 1996 and leave ended on 6 January.

On 13 June there was a Naval Air Command chaplains' meeting at which the future cover for the squadrons at *Osprey* was discussed. I offered to stay on and look after the squadrons until they moved but that was turned down. The chaplains at Yeovilton would provide the cover and would travel back and forth.

Amport Week commenced on 24 June and it was my last. I had had many very happy times at Amport and would miss these occasions. My mind went back to the chaplains I'd met who had graced Amport with their presence and whose stories I had listened to as they 'held court' at the 'Mucky Duck'. But nothing lasts forever.

On my return to Portland I had to prepare for the '*Foylebank*' service. This was a service in memory of sailors from the merchant Service who died in the attack on SS *Foylebank* when she was moored in Portland harbour in 1940. 'Stuka' dive bombers attacked and sank her. It was hard to visualise such a thing happening in the peaceful waters of the harbour. The service duly took place on 7 July at 1200 with a wreath laying at 1300 followed by lunch with the survivors. It was a very moving occasion.

Remembrance Sunday was on the horizon — a big occasion on Portland, shared between local clergy. I got on well with the local incumbent and had taken services for him so that he could have a holiday. Only the week before I had preached at the 'Bible' Sunday service in the parish church. There was a big parade and many wreaths were laid with a civic reception afterwards.

On 12 November I went on retreat at Hillfield Priory, the Franciscan house in Dorset. It gave me a few days for prayer, thought and a chance to re-charge the batteries as it were. The food did not do much to help as it was awful but the brothers were kind and very helpful in their understanding and spiritual direction but I still was undecided as to my future.

My last Sunday service was on 15 December (Advent 3) but the *Osprey* Carol Service took place the following day. On 20 December we went to Christmas Leave.

My very last services in *Osprey* were the Midnight Mass on Christmas Eve and the 1030 Christmas Morning Eucharist and Carols, neither of which were well attended. Going out with a whimper rather than a bang.

We returned from leave on 6 January and a short handover began on 8 January. My relief was Ian Eglin who was one of the chaplains at Yeovilton and would be coming down to *Osprey* once a week (maybe!). During handover I took the opportunity to thank and say farewell to the squadrons and base staff including the staff of the Fitness Centre.

On Thursday 9 January I travelled to Portsmouth for

a final call on the Chaplain of the Fleet.

On 14 January I called on the Captain and thanked him for all his support and kindness, handed in my ID card and various passes and went on terminal leave for four weeks. During this time the hectic work of preparing to hand back the lovely married quarter that I had lived in for the last two years and move to a rectory began. I would miss Weymouth, it is such a lovely town in an equally lovely county. I was going to somewhere very different but by and large people are the same no matter where you go.

Epilogue

Not Quite the End

I left the Royal Navy for the second and last time on Tuesday 14 January 1997 when my final leave ended. I was very sorry to leave but it was inevitable, sooner or later it all had to happen, nothing lasts forever and all good things come to an end.

Well, not quite. I hadn't been in my new parish for long when I received a phone call from my very good friend, Brian Thorne. Brian had joined the Naval Reserve as a 17- year-old signals rating but now he was the commanding officer of *HMS Cambria,* my old stamping ground.

In the intervening years, the chaplain's branch of the Naval Reserve had been disbanded as a cost saving measure but, Brian asked me to become the 'chaplain' to *Cambria* in an unofficial capacity. 'We can't pay you,' he said 'as we have no budget but we'd love to see you and it seems a pity to waste all that experience.' I said that I'd be delighted to return subject to the approval of the Chaplain of the Fleet and the Bishop of Llandaff. Both gave their permission and I took up the mantle of 'Chaplain' to *HMS Cambria* once again. I began visiting the establishment on a once a month basis and continued to do so for the next 18 years. But that too has come to an end and that role is now fulfilled by Father Ben Andrews who is doing an absolutely tremendous job as well as running an extremely busy benefice.

I have shared the lives of some wonderful people, and visited some amazing places all courtesy of the taxpayer so I would like to offer my thanks to all those people who pay taxes enabling me to have those experiences.

I like to think that some of the work that I did would bear fruit but that's the problem with chaplaincy work you rarely see your efforts come to fruition. In a parish a priest could baptise a baby, watch the child grow have the child confirmed and then conduct the wedding of the child and then baptise that child's children. There is a long-term continuity or there used to be. But in chaplaincy work that is not the case. You may bump into people or touch base with them from time to time but in truth, our contact with most people is on a temporary basis. Nevertheless, I would hope that we were able to promote the Christian Faith in difficult circumstances and surroundings to the very people that the church needs most, the young.

It was a privilege to work with those young people who, of course like me, are not so young anymore. But there is a generation coming up behind and I hope that the chaplains who serve with them today are also as fortunate as I was.

So I would like to say 'thank you' to the people who touched my life and whose life I touched; I would like to say 'thank you' to those who served with me who were kind and considerate and again I would like to thank my fellow chaplains who were courteous and kind to me at all times. I had a wonderful time and there was a great deal of laughter and some sorrow but mostly laughter but now it was time to 'turn the page'. As I said to a friend of mine, also a chaplain, 'We are very privileged in some ways because at the very time that most men are thinking of retirement, we move on to new challenges and new opportunities.' So as the Navy 'door' closed behind me the parish 'door' opened.

Opening that particular door was to lead to even more work but of a very different kind. The Parish of Dowlais was part of an area which had been neglected for years. There had been little inward investment and it looked very down at heel but the people were marvellous and we worked hard and because they put their faith in me and I in them and all of us in God, together we were to achieved the building of a new church and a community hall attached to the church and watched the congregation grow.

I moved on to other parishes in Somerset where fundraising for mediaeval churches was hard work too but we did it and again we watched the congregations grow. So as I look back on those years I feel such a great gratitude to God who guided me even though I could not see it and even to this day I find that a God who knows me has got to be incredibly tolerant.

Thanks to you too for reading this book I hope you

enjoyed it, I hope you can forgive my self-indulgence but it was never a matter of ego rather a desire to share a story, principally with my grandson who is too young to read it but I hope one day he will. I hope the story, a part of my life, was and will continue to be worthwhile. God bless you and I pray that He who guided me, even though I did not know it, will guide you too.

Acknowledgements

Having mentioned that John Tolhurst and I served together three times I was delighted that he agreed to write the foreword to this book. He is a very busy man and I am deeply grateful that his comments add some gravitas to this work.

In football much is made of a goal scoring forward but the rest of the team contributes otherwise no goal! So it is with a book. I could not have done this without help from many quarters, so a very big thank you to Stephanie Chilman who once again has guided and advised me with patience and wisdom based on her vast experience. Once again I am indebted to Bogna Zegradska for her delightful work in the design of the cover which followed closely in style to the first book but with great skill she has managed to age me! My sister-in-law Philippa has once again provided sterling help in proofreading the manuscript and always there is my wife, Laura, encouraging, advising and providing very constructive criticism as well as reading through and correcting the manuscript.

I am grateful too to a number of friends who provided information which moved the narrative along and to Gary McKenzie and Guy Tolhurst through whose good offices I was able to contact Captain John.

Thank you too dear reader for reading this book which is based on memory so any errors are mine and mine alone.

Finally, I would like to thank the men and women whose lives I shared, albeit briefly and whose company I so enjoyed. I hope that I served and ministered to them in the way they deserved. My grateful thanks to the Royal Navy for providing me with employment which enriched my life and for the kind permission to use the photographs of the ships and crests which mean so much to me.

Michael Wishart
June 2022

Printed in Great Britain
by Amazon